"Our Christian reporters had their shields dented with armour-piercing cloves of fire—coming from the mouth of God, or was it from the pit of fire?"

Ruben Ortega

The interviewers were young and bright. They were sympathetic to the Jesus Movement.

The responses are unusually dependable.

From up and down the West Coast and across the nation comes this sampling of beliefs voiced by Jesus People to peers—uninhibited responses—gleaned as interviewer and interviewee rapped about ideas important to them both.

"Why such a book?" How many times have you asked, "What do Jesus People believe?" "Is their faith real?" "Is this Movement of God?" "Will it last?"

Now you can hear from the Jesus People themselves just what they think and practice. You can judge for yourself.

A graduate of Berkeley, Ruben Ortega has been in the center of campus turmoil in recent years. The perspective he brings to this book is that of a campus activist—he made an unsuccessful, but heralded, bid for student body president at the University of California at Berkeley when he was a senior—and a minority group heritage—he's a California Chicano.

He and his wife Carolyn have one young daughter. Staff members have living quarters in the apartment house which serves as headquarters for Collegiate Encounter with Christ.

Ortega, who turned down scholarships from several outstanding law schools when he graduated from Berkeley, works with a staff of 25 young zealots (some of them still students—one a member of the Berkeley Senate—some veterans of Christian World Liberation Front) to witness to students, street people, and servicemen in the San Francisco Bay Area.

Because he's in the Bay Area and on the streets, Ruben's insights are valuable and his copy is authentic.

The Jesus People Speak Out!

COMPILED BY RUBEN ORTEGA

PYRAMID BOOKS • NEW YORK

THE JESUS PEOPLE SPEAK OUT!

A Pyramid Book
Published by arrangement with
David C. Cook Publishing Company

Pyramid edition published April, 1972

Pyramid Books are published by Pyramid Communications, Inc.
Its trademarks, consisting of the word "Pyramid" and the
portrayal of a pyramid, are registered in the United States
Patent Office.

PYRAMID COMMUNICATIONS, INC.
919 Third Avenue
New York, New York 10022, U.S.A.

CONTENTS

INTRODUCTION

We've heard about the Jesus Movement, the apparent enthusiasm.

We've seen their stickers on subway walls, sidewalks, tollroad pay booths, sides of buildings.

We know they're there. But what do they really believe and how are they different from other young people in and out of the church?

Countless thousands across our country have asked questions of their bishops, ministers, and priests. People want to know. Is this Movement legitimate Christianity, or another abortive fad? Is it truly a revolutionary happening? Or is it a counter-culture, dissatisfied with a no-solution society, just using a new way to express itself?

Armed with 25 tape recorders, 15 typewriters, and 100 roles of recording tape, my staff and I set out to find from the Jesus People themselves what they believe and to determine if the press and countless authors have been accurate in their interpretations of the Movement.

The entire staff of Collegiate Encounter with Christ, our Christian group of collegians and college graduates, left their assigned jobs on the junior college campuses of northern California and roamed the San Andreas Fault in search of insights into the spiritual quake that has been shaking our country. They wanted answers—not to condemn, nor to condone, but to inform.

We found the Jesus people we interviewed on the streets, pedaling *Truth* (a Movement newspaper), in their communes, at their coffee shops, in their Bible studies.

Since the Jesus Movement began in California, it is fitting, with a few exceptions, that the interviews be conducted in that state. Our staff tried to get a good cross-California coverage, and we feel that the people interviewed are well representative of the popular, or semi-popular Movement.

In no way can this book provide all the answers. The reader—clergy or layman—must inform himself, arrive at his own conclusions, and from them decide what he should do.

—Ruben Ortega

"UNLESS A MAN FORSAKE ALL THAT
HE HATH, HE CANNOT BE MY DISCIPLE."
BATTLE CRY—(CHILDREN OF GOD).

Chapter 1

A NEW MOVEMENT FOR JESUS?

Has anyone, or can anyone define exactly what the Jesus Movement really is? When we talked to those in the Movement we were amazed at their answers.

What is the Jesus Movement?

"I really don't feel that I am a part of the Jesus Movement. When people say, 'the Jesus Movement,' it sounds like the Black Panther movement or just another movement that has come, and another movement that is going to go. If you take the word *movement* off and just leave the word Jesus on, then you have got something." *Barry, Berkeley, California.*

"I don't really believe that there is a Jesus Movement separate from the Body of Christ. It's a label given to Christians, especially those who are young."
Howard, Alameda, California.

"Right now, it's mostly studying and preaching the Kingdom to whom we can here, and we have meetings; and we're trying to experience, and God's trying to work through us; He's getting us ready, chastising us and dragging us through the mud to take us to the cross, take us to a hill and put us in a place where He can use us." *Rich, Maranatha House.*

What is the goal of the Jesus Movement as it relates to individuals?

"I think the goal is, first of all, to show these kids that Jesus is real and alive and doing well, contrary to popular belief." *Chuck.*

"To get as many people right with God before they go to hell." *Ken, Spokane, Washington, Maranatha.*

"I think that God's goal is more important than what our goal is. God's goal is to bring the Body together in one mind and one accord, believing the same doctrine and the same worship. Also, I think that God's goal is also to bring us into perfect Koinonia, which means 'in a Greek fellowship,' a perfect commune with each other."

Nancy, San Jose, California, Agape House.

What is the goal of the Jesus Movement concerning the United States?

"Right now, I think our mission is to reach America, you know, the United States, because this is our country and our country was brought up in the name of God. Like in our Pledge of Allegiance it says, 'under God'; and on our coins, 'In God We Trust.' But yet, we're turning our backs on God, and it's really sad. There's a Scripture, I think it's 2 Numbers 7: 14. It says, 'If my people, who are called by My name, will humble themselves and pray, then I will hear, forgive them their sins, and heal their lands.' So that, I think, is really our mission."

Shauna, Fresno, California, Agape Force.

"We want to see America change, although it seems hopeless at times. We believe in the last days that God will pour out His spirit on all mankind. I believe it is beginning. People say that the Jesus Movement is a fad; I don't believe it. Maybe some of it is and some of it isn't, but our main goals are to see America change —cities change—and we have seen cities change. We believe that when the revival comes, cities change and countries change."

Dan, Los Angeles, California, Agape Force.

Does the Jesus Movement have any world-view goals?

"I believe the goals of the Jesus Movement are to fulfill the Great Commission given in Mark 16: 15. In Acts 1: 8, first they started in Jerusalem, Judea, and Samaria and then they went into the uttermost parts of the world. Christians started out as a little nucleus around Los Angeles and San Francisco and then it went around the United States and now it's spreading out into the world."

Dan, Merced, California, Christian House.

"The goal of this Movement is to reach the whole world for Christ."

Sheila, Santa Barbara, California, Children of God.

"I feel that in my heart, that in searching the Acts Church out, that more Christians should dedicate more and more of their life, more and more of their stuff to getting this Church moving that's being started right now. I think that this Church that is being started right now is not a building church, but is the real Body of Christ. I think that it is not only started in California but it is all over the world right now."

Dan, Santa Rosa, California, Rapping Post.

"When Christ gave us the Great Commission, He told us to go out into the world and to witness for Him and to baptize people in the name and power of the Holy Ghost, to be an evangelist and to get the Word out."

Doug, Richmond, California.

Is the Jesus Movement growing or dissolving?

"The Movement will never dissolve."

Dennis, Turlock, California, Christian House.

11

"I believe the Jesus Movement is dissolving. There was a tremendous revival, and a lot of people jumped in. And God is expecting people now to follow on in what they know; there's not all the fun and the excitement any more. A lot of people are falling away. A lot of people are falling into heresy; there's all kinds of junk going."

C. G., Mill Valley, California, Ivy House.

"This Movement is nothing new—it's been going on for 2,000 years, and Christ is coming back. He said that in the last days He would pour out His Spirit upon all flesh, so this Movement isn't going to dissolve because you can't stop the work of the Lord."

Troy, Atwater, California, The Christian House.

"Sometimes it is a fad. I think with people it depends on whether or not you last. If you don't stick with it, it's just a fad. As far as this outpouring of the Spirit, that's a different thing. God's pouring His Spirit out and showing people that He loves them. He manifests Himself to people, and that isn't exactly a fad." *Harry, Carmel, California.*

"I think it is going to dissolve and the ones who really did make that commitment in their hearts are going to be the only ones left out of the Movement."

Ken, Spokane, Washington, Maranatha.

"The Movement can dissolve—and I know it is— that's not really the point. God couldn't find a lot of people that He could use so He had to go to a lot of the young people; the hippies; all these drug users; just plain people; high school and college kids. And God had to raise them up, and He started a big Movement. This Movement, I believe, is going to die and we're going to be left with a very strong church."

Rich, Campbell, California, Maranatha House.

Would you use the phrase, "Getting high on Jesus"?

"I wouldn't use that word 'high.' You talk to somebody and you say, 'Why don't you get high on Jesus?' And they'll think it's something like dope or something. There's been times I've been 'low' on Jesus."
Carol, San Francisco, California.

"I think it is man trying to sell Jesus on the same level as a drug addict trying to compare Jesus to a high. I think it's selling Jesus short."
Anonymous, Texas.

"I don't like using that term anymore because it isn't a high. It's a reality, the reality of Jesus with man. It's peace inside of you."
Joel, Hillsborough, California.

"Most people that use this term 'getting high on Jesus' are the ones that come out of a drug background. A lot of them don't really realize what they're saying. I don't feel that it is a very good term to use. Jesus isn't a high; He's reality. I believe the words shouldn't be used."
Martin, Campbell, California, House of Uttering.

"I've experienced getting super-high on Jesus, and my husband has, and he's been in a lot of drugs before he came, and he says, 'It's just a super-high; it's really neat.' "
Mildred, Los Angeles, California.

"Getting high on Jesus is really having faith in Jesus, and it just really freaks your mind out just knowing that you have so much power, and you never have to be afraid of anything."
Shelley, San Mateo, California.

"Personally, I don't use the term 'getting high on Jesus.' This is something that the media has picked up and has made a big deal of. The apostle Paul says, 'Don't be drunk with wine, but be filled with the Holy Spirit.' When a person is filled with the Holy Spirit, if that person is emotional by nature, he might experience some emotion—just like if he's emotional at some basketball game he may cheer a little hard. The same way with religion. It depends on the person's temperament."   *Anonymous.*

"I guess when you say, 'getting high,' you think of feeling good and everything is all right; and when you're a Christian you have joy deep inside, even when everything outside isn't all right. You can still feel good and know it'll turn out. When you're a Christian you have hope, so I guess in that way you are high."   *Sandra, Sunnyvale, California.*

"Definitely. So much more real than drugs or alcohol—it's very uplifting and there's no comedown. That's the thing I like about it most."
                          Gary, Menlo Park, California.

"I use the term 'getting high on Jesus' because it is similar to the temporary state I had when I used drugs. I laid my burden on the Lord when I came to the Lord and He took it away. The feeling that I got when I was on drugs was what got my mind away from all my problems and all that, but now that I know the Lord, it's not so much the feeling as just the believing —the knowing about God's love and His promises that get me high (so to speak)."
Rekum, Hayward, California, Leader Children of God.

Is a Jesus "high" a good feeling?

"It's definitely a good feeling. Getting high on Jesus is something that is beyond trying to explain. We can get hung up in that and say that that is just an emotional experience, but when Jesus Christ is living in your life, and He is answering the questions of your life, and supplying your needs, it's beyond understanding. It blows your mind."

Amy, San Martin, California, Teen Challenge.

"Yeah, it's a good feeling. It's a good feeling to have eternal peace running through you—to know that you're going to live forever, to know that God's real."

Ken, Spokane, Washington, Maranatha.

"Yes, there is a good feeling and there's a feeling that goes 24 hours a day; it's always there."

Anonymous, Texas.

"Well, be careful when you start going by feelings. Because once that feeling has gone away, you are going to think you have lost the whole thing."

Anonymous.

"I don't like the term, 'getting high on Jesus,' because it's more than a high and feelings aren't all. I believe that a Christian should live by faith and by Jesus' statements."   *Howard, Alameda, California.*

"I don't think emotions play any part at all. In the past when I first became a Christian I based a lot of it on emotions. Since then when I talked to people about becoming Christians I've tried to carefully explain to them that emotions really play no part—that Christ is with us always; if we wake up one morning feeling bad, that He is still with us. Christ isn't a high."

Phil, San Mateo, California.

Aren't there difficulties in this type of a Movement?

"There's bad in every movement there is; and the only good anywhere in anything is Jesus Christ in it, and it's gonna be corrupted by the men working in it and Satan. I don't know of any organization anywhere; but where there's people there's gonna be corruption. In the church there's gonna be bad; there's bad in everybody." *George, Jacksonville, Illinois, His House.*

"They've lost Jesus Christ in the Movement. They really don't know what they're moving towards."
Mark, Portland, Oregon.

"There are a lot of people who have come to know Christ, but on a superficial level. It's like if Satan could water-down a Christian, he'll do it in any way he can, and get them off on strange doctrines. Consequently, a lot of 'Jesus Freaks' are taking it like a trip, whereas they don't know Jesus in the deeper sense of the word, because when you know Jesus He reveals all things to you. And right now, since we are in the Last Days, there are many factions working against the pure Christian."
Kyle, Berkeley, California, Resurrection City.

"I feel that any young, over-zealous Christian, who is not established in a doctrine, has a tendency to very often, one way or the other, either fall into the trap of either too legalistic, either too much under the law, or too much under grace."
Dan, Santa Rosa, California, Rapping Post.

"Yes, often times people really give their lives to Jesus, but Satan can come in as Jesus—in the name of Jesus—and lead them astray."
Eugene, New York, New York.

"We're meeting the needs of people here in Berkeley—which is the radical; the drug addict; just the different movements and the different things that are represented here. There's about five or six Christian organizations here and I believe that in Christ there is a unity between Christians and it is very truly needed, and it says that the judgment begins with the Body of

Christ; they begin in the House of God. Before we can go forth and really preach the Gospel and really represent Christ in a true way, we really have to look at ourselves and also form a unity among the other Christians. We haven't been very successful in this, I guess. It could be our own pride."

Kathy, Texas, Resurrection City.

"I think a few things that are wrong in the Christian gossip line is 'getting high on Jesus' and 'tripping' for Jesus."

Martin, Campbell, California, House of Uttering.

What is a Jesus Freak anyway?

"I think if anyone calls himself a 'Jesus Freak' or considers himself being part of the Jesus Movement, that they're really fleshly, they're really immature in the Lord, and that they're not serving God according to His will and they're not being led by the Holy Spirit." *Ken, Spokane, Washington, Maranatha House.*

"Jesus Freaks—a person that goes around wearing crazy things and carrying a big Bible; Christian that isn't intelligent." *Sandra, Sunnyvale, California.*

"People that call themselves Jesus Freaks or Christians, I don't think really are at all. They have the appearance of being a Christian, and they do the things they think that Christians are supposed to do, but they aren't really Christians at all."

Debbie, Massachusetts, Maranatha House.

Are there individuals or groups within the Jesus Movement who are causing problems?

"Reincarnated Pharisees." *Byron, Miami, Florida.*

"I'm not going to name any names because it isn't really important. I think if we have any relationship

17

with Christ and we really know Him as a Friend, we'll know when somebody isn't telling the truth about Him—not telling how it really is."

Steve, Mountain View, California.

"Any Christian organization that practices spiritism —it would be nice to stay away from them."

Stephen, Alameda, California, The Way.

"There are supposedly a group around New York of Jesus Freaks, and around Big Sur who call themselves Jesus Freaks, but are actually witchcraft."

Danny, Redwood City, California, House of Manna.

"There are a few cults that borrow from the Bible and take parts of it; and then other parts they reject. I believe that some of these are the Jehovah's Witnesses, Mormons, Bahai's—people like this."

Ben, Vallejo, California, New Disciples of Jesus.

"Some people say that it's really important to raise your hands in praise. And if you don't do that it shows that you're resisting the Spirit. With me, I don't see anything wrong with raising your hands but if it's going to make other people stumble then I'll do it in private. Also, some require certain things I've never seen required in the Bible."

Steve, Berkeley, California.

"There's a lot of people in the mountains that believe they were called to be in the mountains, because there's a Scripture that says, 'Those in the valley will flee to the mountains of Judea,' and they believe that this part of Oregon is Judea."

Rich, Campbell, California, Maranatha House.

"I've heard of one, the Children of God around here. I don't know what they're really like. There's another one up in Santa Cruz. I don't know the exact name of them, but they're walking around as Jesus

18

People, and you talk to them and they've got hatred in their hearts. You can see it in the whole group."

Gary, San Francisco, California.

"It seems I have witnessed accounts and talked to these people; it seems that they are being possessed with something controlling them and they really don't know what they are doing. It's kind of like they are tramps of some sort. I think this is extremely dangerous and must be discerned immediately and dealt with." *Doug, Richmond, California.*

"There is a Family of God place in Texas with a fence around the whole thing, and you're forced to stay. The doctrine not only is wrong, but Scripturally it is morally wrong. There are many others, people who are walking around professing that they are Christians, and churches also; and the Scriptures say that there are many people around professing to be Christians who really aren't."

Nick, Turlock, California, Leader of His House.

"Satan's strategy is to undercut what Jesus is doing, and the greatest thing, I believe, is happening today among the people in the Jesus Movement—so Satan immediately tries to counterfeit what God is genuinely doing. People who are involved in Satan worship, witchcraft, demonism and things like this take on religious overtones and become a false Jesus Freak. So in one sense Satan comes through with Eastern religions and calls this Jesus. In the other sense, he comes through with people who believe the Bible, but only believe a portion of it. And Satan's strategy, I believe, to undercut the Jesus Movement, is to take truth and twist it just slightly." *Anonymous.*

"The Children of God, but I can't make any judgments. It's just that they have Jesus but they . . . I don't know about them." *Byron, Miami, Florida*

19

"The only thing that comes to my mind is a group called the Children of God. They are the type of zealots who take the Bible out of context. Like, hate your mother and your father. And they don't work because they don't feel they should. They would go into churches and bust up services."

Gary, Redwood City, California.

"Well, I've heard of the Children of God, and stuff like that. I think that a lot of them are good to the extent where they know their Bible inside and out, and that's good; but a lot of the things they take out of context. They have an idea, and they take something out of the Bible and they conform that to their idea. I really admire the dedication that they do have and the obedience that they do have. But, they're just based on bitterness and hatred."

Debbie, Massachusetts, Maranatha House.

What is your objective as a part of the Jesus Movement?

"Right now I'm not too interested in saving souls, I used to be. I'm more interested in finding peace."

Rick, Carmel, California.

"My goal is to serve God and put Him first. I don't want a big house. I want to live an easy life and not try to make it to the top." *Steve, Berkeley, California.*

"I want to tell, at least let everybody know about Christ, you know, so that they can choose for themselves." *Alicia, San Francisco, California*

"My goal is, like I said before, to get 49,152 dedicated Christians, taking those people with willing hearts; teaching them and guiding them in the way of the Lord; seeing that their needs are met, one by one, on a multiplication basis."

Nick, Turlock, California, Leader of His House.

"It would be to tell people about the Gospel, which is the love of God that He has for them."
Teresa, San Mateo, California, The Way In Coffee House.

"I can't talk about my goals because they are the Lord's goals. I am dead to myself, my goals no longer exist. The Lord's goals are to get His people ready so He can come." *Steve, Mountain View, California.*

"Well, what I would like is for more people to know Christ, especially my friends. It would be kind of nice if it was a Christ-filled world. And peace, that I don't think will ever happen because of human nature."
Kristal, San Mateo, California.

Where do you expect to be 5-10 years from now?

"It becomes a burden on your flesh to try and figure out what you're going to do tomorrow."
Dan, Santa Rosa, California, Rapping Post.

"Serving God."
Cornelius, Dallas, Texas, Children of God.

"I expect to be where the Lord will have me. I hope I am exactly on schedule."
Doug, Richmond, California.

"I expect to be sharing Christ in the best way I know how. That's the exciting thing. You always know where you're going—you never need to worry about it because God's taking me there and I'll be doing whatever He wants." *Mark, Portland, Oregon.*

"I really can't say. I believe that God is doing a tremendous work in Berkeley, and I believe that we may move on to another area, even though we will always have a work in Berkeley." *Anonymous.*

"As far as ten years from now? In Heaven."
Nick, Turlock, California, Leader of His House.

"With the Lord, I hope, Brother."
Robert, Portland, Oregon.

"Well, the Rapture could come at any time; I expect to be with Jesus." *Anonymous.*

"I'm hoping the Lord will come before then, but if He doesn't, I'll do whatever He wants me to do."
Anonymous.

"If I'm not in Heaven, I'll be in the position God gives me." *Rich, Maranatha.*

"In five years I hope to be finished with college. I hope to become a nurse and to go to Africa or some place like that." *Kristal, San Mateo, California.*

"I don't know exactly, but I sort of think I'll live in another country being a nurse, or something like that." *Sandra, Sunnyvale, California.*

"I will probably be married to some evangelist."
Terry, Redwood City, California.

"I haven't thought that far ahead."
Danny, Redwood City, House of Manna.

What would you do if the Jesus Movement were to dissolve?

"I don't depend on the Jesus Movement. In a sense, I don't feel that I have anything to do with it, really. My life isn't depending on what everyone else does, but on what God wants me to do."
Debbie, San Jose, California, Maranatha House.

"If the Movement ever were to dissolve, I don't believe that would affect my walk with the Lord. It's kind of like, if everyone left in the whole world abandoned God, it wouldn't have any effect on me, because the relationship is with a living God and not a relationship with a Movement."
Sheila, Santa Barbara, California, Children of God.

22

"I expect that it will. I believe prophecy and that there is going to be persecution. A lot of the Movement will dissolve and Christians will no longer be part of it in a physical body. I praise the Lord because it could be very soon."

Steve, Mountain View, California.

"If it be of God, there would be no stopping it. I don't believe it will dissolve. But if it does, I'll still serve Jesus."

Sheila, Santa Barbara, California, Children of God.

"Keep on, because before the Movement I was a Christian. I don't think that just because the Movement dissolves my faith in God will dissolve."

Kristal, San Mateo, California.

"I'd either join another movement or give up on the world and try to live in my spirit completely."

Byron, Miami, Florida.

"I would just pray that the Lord would send something to take its place. Look at the early church: they were busted up but the Lord took care of them."

Micky, New Jersey.

"Well, the Movement can't dissolve. That's the deal. If you're talking about a people movement, then yes, it can dissolve. But if we're talking about Jesus Christ working through people, then it can never dissolve. It's impossible. It's impregnant."

Mark, Portland, Oregon.

"I have my own personal relationship with Jesus Christ. Everybody else (and I know a lot of people do) has their own personal relationship with Jesus Christ. If their relationship dissolves, you know, it's too bad. I don't believe it will. But my personal relationship with Jesus will never dissolve, because He promised." *George, Jacksonville, Florida.*

23

Chapter 2

WHAT DOES IT MEAN TO BE A CHRISTIAN?

What does it mean to be a Christian? An authoritative definition to that question has bothered evangelicals, the neo-orthodox, fundamentalists— everybody in "Christian" circles.

The Jesus Movement has been classified as fundamental. A literal interpretation of the Bible was assumed as their authority in all doctrinal matters.

In reality, the stance of the Jesus People toward orthodox Christianity actually tends to de-emphasize **sin** and **repentance** in favor of love and brotherhood and a new humanitarian world.

Exceptions to this doctrinal tendency are generally witnessed in the non-charismatic groups, such as Christian World Liberation Front, Jesus Light and Power Company, and perhaps a few others.

What is a Christian?

"A Christian is somebody who says he is a Christian."   *Joel, Hillsborough.*

"A believer in God, the Holy Spirit, Jesus Christ."
                    Karen, Richmond, California.

"A Christian is not just a person who goes to church on every Sunday, but a person who really knows Jesus in a real personal way."
                    Tim, Menlo Park, California, House of Manna.

"A Christian is a person who accepts Jesus as his personal Savior into his life."
                    Dennis, Whittier, California, Christian House.

"Well, first of all, you can't be born into it for one thing. I believe that a Christian is somebody that has really experienced, and personally accepted Christ into their lives."   *Vicki, Washington.*

"A Christian is someone who follows Jesus, like me."   *Dan, Merced, California, Christian House.*

"It's that thing of being born of incorruptible seed, which happens the minute you confess the Lord Jesus Christ as your Lord and Savior; that's what makes you a Christian."
                    Steve, Alameda, California, The Way.

"A Christian is an individual who is Christ-like, a person who takes the ideas and precepts of the Bible and applies them to his life and lives by them."
                    Dan, Redwood City, California.

"There are two types of Christians: there is the American Christian and there are those who believe in Jesus Christ. A Christian is one who follows the Word of God and obeys it and reads it."
                    Anonymous, Rochester, New York.

"A Christian is someone who spends his ability as a mortal fleshly person following the theology and the doctrine set down by the Savior Christ."

Bill, San Pablo, California.

"Someone who knows Christ, someone who manifests Christ, not someone who talks about Christ but manifests Him."

Neil, Detroit, Michigan, Still Water Store.

"Well, a Christian, I guess, is a person who has accepted Jesus Christ into their life and attempts to follow the teachings He laid down in the Bible in his daily life, and would lay down his life for his brother."

Susan, Minneapolis, Minnesota.

"A disciple is a Christian—one who forsakes all for Christ." *Cornelius, Dallas, Texas, Children of God.*

"One who serves God. A believer is one who has Jesus in his heart."

Rekum, Hayward, California, Leader of Children of God.

"Someone who wants to be like Christ, to follow Christ."

Debby, Campbell, California, Maranatha House.

"I think it's just a person who loves God, who follows His ways, is holy—kind of like Christ."

Gary, Menlo Park, California.

"A Christian is someone who has surrendered his life to God. He has put away earthly possessions and earthly desires of the flesh."

Martin, California, Maranatha House.

"*Christian* is derived from the word disciple; they were called Christians at the church of Antioch. Acts 12: 26."

Daniel, Campbell, California, Leader of Maranatha House.

"I'm still trying to define that. A Christian is one who truly acknowledges Christ as Lord and who tries as best he can."

Barry, Berkeley, California.

"Somebody who believes in God and tries to help other people become Christians, and shares his faith with people and brings them closer to the Lord and explains what He's all about and everything like that."

Richard, Turlock, California, Rapping Post.

"A man who believes God. A guy who does the Lord's will. And a guy who can forgive someone seventy times seven, like God said. A man who walks down the street, and people can make fun of him and push him in the gutter and more to come. And the Lord said that you can be a real man in His eyes."

Chuck.

"I would say that a true Christian is not only one who hears the Word of Jesus but who lives it and feels it. I say there are many people who believe in Jesus Christ, believe in God, who kill people out of greed for money, who hate people, who are on so many evil trips, who on Sunday go to church, very pious; and to me they're no better than the Pharisees at the time of Christ."

Eugene, New York, New York.

"Christianity as far as I'm concerned is God Himself, the Spirit of God—that's Christianity; God's Spirit walking on this earth."

Mike, Salt Lake City, Utah.

Where should a Christian worship?

"You should worship where you're at because ye are the temple of God."

Eric, San Mateo, California, Brothers House.

"I think a Christian can worship almost any place that he feels that God is near him but I think the established church is a very good thing to have, and he can worship by singing and praying and dancing— whatever he thinks will honor God."

Dan, Turlock, California, Rapping Post.

"You can worship in church, you can worship at home, it doesn't really matter. You can be in a constant state of prayer as you're going to work and back, and it doesn't really matter where it is."

Ben, Vallejo, California, New Disciples of Jesus.

"I worship God in a lot of different places: in my bed, in church, or walking down the street. It doesn't matter, but we can glorify Him in song and Spirit."

John, Whittier, California.

"Wherever you are—say you're in a park; say you're at home. I mean you know—your body's God's temple."

Eugene, New York, New York.

How should a Christian worship?

"I think a Christian should worship God in the best way they think is right, from what they know."

Mildred, Los Angeles, California.

"With all of His mind, body and soul, in whatever way he feels comfortable. If he likes standing on his head, fine. Loud or quiet, it doesn't matter. Whatever form his worship takes, he should do it with all of himself." *Amy, San Martin, California.*

"The Bible says that God is a spirit and that we must worship Him in truth and in deed."

Maoch, Southern California, Children of God.

"In his own way; you know there are different ways to worship God. You can worship God singing a song, you know. Like we speak in tongues and stuff like that. We kind of get loose in the Spirit."

Joe, San Leandro, California, Drug Abuse Preventive Center.

"By praying. Myself, I pray and before you know it the Spirit of God comes."

Carol, San Francisco, California.

"A real Christian worships God in the things that he does—preaching the Gospel, leading people to Christ —going to all the world and preaching the Gospel is true worship."

Cornelius, Dallas, Texas, Children of God.

"I think that everything you do should be an active worship to the Lord. I really like audible praise and audible worship, speaking in tongues, is really important in worshiping the Lord."   *Anonymous.*

"In prayer. There's different types of worship. The Bible tells us there is nine kinds of ways to worship the Lord; lifting of the hands, dancing, clapping, singing; just a joyful noise unto the Lord."

Rick, San Jose, California, Maranatha House.

"Worship generates spiritual power, and this can be directed either towards Satan or towards God. Sometimes here at church, when God's power is really powerful, people have been known to dance in the Spirit, just because they are worshiping God with their heart, with their mind, with their soul, and even with their body."   *Shelley, San Mateo, California.*

"In spirit, like in Psalms it talks about lifting up holy hands without wrath or doubting, clapping your hands, singing, dancing, weeping."

Ann, San Jose, California, Maranatha House.

29

What do Jesus People feel about the established church?

"I think a church is really helpful for most people, because they have a leader there who knows the Bible, and can help them learn and understand."   *Alicia.*

"In a church I find the fellowship, and there I can hear the Word of God and I will admit that there's hypocrites in churches, but I myself have seen examples of hypocrisy in my own life and I try my best to work it out through Christ."

Kathy, Texas, Resurrection City.

"There is no church, group, or organization doing God's perfect will. Every man is my superior in some way. There is something I can learn from everyone."
Dan, Merced, California, Christian House.

"Jesus called the established church the synagogue of Satan. They are not of God. Because I went to church all my life and I never met Jesus. And I've been to many churches all over the country, and they weren't Christ-like at all."

Cornelius, Dallas, Texas, Children of God.

"I know there's a lot of churches that they only go to to show off their cars, to do the social trips, and God's not pleased with them at all. There's a lot of churches that need to do a lot of heavy repenting."
Ken, Spokane, Washington, Maranatha House.

". . . the institutionalized church, in my eyes, is something completely different from the church, the Body of Christ. I think the institutionalized church is much like a government, a world system government. The institutionalized church today seems to be continuously going downhill and the decisions and resolutions that they're coming up with prove all the more their state of corruption."

Doug, Richmond, California.

"There is a lot of lip service going on, and people sit in churches and open their hymnals and sing and pray, but God says that in the flesh we cannot please Him. Our worship is to be done from the inner man, not just because it is a socially accepted thing."

Debbie, San Jose, California, Maranatha.

"90% of the churches are wrong, but nevertheless, that doesn't mean that God doesn't use them. I believe the Lord's going to bring all the Christians together, into one Church of His Body which is spoken of in the Bible."

Daniel, San Jose, California, Maranatha House.

"The Bible says that God dwells not in temples made with human hands but in peoples' hearts. And a lot of people don't realize this and they think that you can find God in church. I'm not saying that you can't; you can, but I think that Christ is best in a person's life." *Gary, Redwood City, California, Maranatha.*

What do you think about the Bible?

"I think that the Bible is the inspired Word of God and that it definitely has a place in our lives if we are going to be Christians."

Anonymous.

"II Timothy 3: 16 and 17 says that the whole Bible was given to us by inspiration of God, is useful to teach us what is wrong in our lives and help us out and makes us realize."

Nick, Turlock, California, Leader of His House.

"The best way that I know to grow in the knowledge of God is to get into the Bible—just to really get into it. It has to be personal study."

George, Jacksonville, Illinois, Leader of His House.

31

"Some of the groups just don't have the full truth. If they won't accept the full truth, the Lord will show them. The full truth is the full Bible as it is written, not in private interpretation or anything like this."

Maoch, Southern California, Children of God.

"You don't need man's wisdom, all you need is the wisdom of God which is contained in the Bible. To get that all you need to do is to know how to read, and to do that all you need is the Bible."   *Anonymous.*

Do you believe in witnessing?

"I went to the streets and spoke about Jesus and the ones who listened the most were the youth who had experimented with dope, booze, sex, or just materialism and were willing to do anything to get meaning into their lives."   *Ron.*

"I think you should move as the Spirit leads. I think you should present the Gospel of Jesus Christ to everybody. Everyone you see could go to hell at any time and if by you, that person is kept from going to Hell then I don't think we should take chances."

Ken, Spokane, Washington, Maranatha House.

Are you dogmatic in presenting your beliefs to others?

"I think we should be very dogmatic in presenting the truth of Jesus Christ. But while we're presenting our beliefs we should be very understanding of the other person."   *Micky, New Jersey.*

"I believe we can be no more or less dogmatic than what is set down in the Word of God."

Doug, Richmond, California.

"It is a world of sin we live in today and I think we should be dogmatic about it."

Robert, Portland, Oregon.

"One should be dogmatic in the sense that they know exactly what they believe; they know exactly what's of God. In dealing with other people, you have to look at that person and understand exactly where they are, and exactly what they need to be told where they are. Dogma is kind of a funny word. When you know truth, you can't compromise it. But when you don't know something for sure, don't say you do."

C. G., Mill Valley, California, Ivy House.

How should you witness to others to be most effective?

"Give it all you got. Any way, shape, form, or manner . . . for Jesus Christ. Use T.V., radio, newspapers, knock on doors, do anything you want to."

Anonymous, Rochester, New York.

"Well, you can't really force it on them. I think that you should let the Lord do it. You've got to deal with people differently. Some people you've got to deal with gently and some people you have to deal with in other ways."

Debbie, Massachusetts, Maranatha House.

"I believe you should present Jesus Christ not as a belief, but as a way of life." *Anonymous.*

"The most important thing, I feel, is to confront the kids 'eyeball to eyeball.' Only then could the barriers be broken down." *John, Jesus Light and Power Co.*

"I think you have to do it in meekness and in love. If it's not in love, then you're just pushing it down someone's throat. I think you have to take care of their need. I think talking about it is good too but you have to be careful because Christians have a problem of talking too much. I think it's better if you keep your mouth shut most of the time." *Rich.*

"You cannot go about and pick the green fruit. Like during my life a lot of times I was approached by a Jesus believer, a Jesus person, and like I couldn't listen because I was a green fruit."

Mark, Portland, Oregon.

"Well, we should be wise as serpents and harmless as doves. We should be ready at all times to present our faith in an intelligent manner. In some ways we should be bold as lions—in other ways we should be timid and meek. It all depends on the situation."

Anonymous.

"I feel that you shouldn't water down your beliefs; you should present them just the way they are. If you don't, then you just have kids that don't really understand or else they're in it just for a trip and don't really understand it for what it's supposed to be."

Karen, Reedley, California, Agape Force.

"I believe you should win the person over to yourself, make a friend of him and then express your beliefs and just show some love. If he has some beliefs, word it in a way that you have tried other things but this is what you have found that has changed your life."

Joe, Santa Cruz, California, Drug Abuse Prevention Center.

Is there a point where Christianity and other religions meet, and if so, where is that point?

"The only point where Christianity and other religions could meet is in a man's desire to find God. I don't believe that any other religion besides Christianity can show you God. Every other religion besides Christianity has to be based on one of two things: either God is already inside you, and you just have to

34

find God, or God is above you someplace, and by certain things you can do you can reach him. Christianity says that God is not inside you. He is far beyond you and nothing you can ever do can take you there. All you can do is lay down your life, and accept God's life into you by recognizing you're nothing."

John, El Cajon, California.

"You could take away Mohammed out of Mohammedanism and Buddha out of Buddhism, and still have the religions because all they are is legalistic rules. But Jesus Christ is an essential part of Christianity. If you take Jesus Christ out of Christianity, Christianity would cease to exist. And that's why I'd say Christianity would be unique." *Mark, Portland, Oregon.*

"Christianity is God's concept of what man is and should be. Buddha and the other philosophers say, 'I will show you the way to find truth,' and what is good about Jesus is that He says, 'I am the truth, the way, and the life, no man can come to the Father but by me.' So I have to say, no there's no point."

Bob, El Cajon, California.

"No. Whereas Buddha says, 'I am pointing to the light,' other religions are saying, 'I am meditating on myself.' Jesus says, 'Unless you are born again, you will not enter the Kingdom of Heaven,' and 'no man comes to me but that the Father draw him.' All the other religions have been deceived in one form or another. If I gave you 99.9% of the truth, it would still be a lie." *Kyle, Berkeley, California.*

"I think that one thing that distinguishes Christianity from any other religion is God reaching down to man through Jesus Christ, and all other religions or philosophies or whatever is man's attempt to reach God or find the answer somewhere in nature or within himself." *Troy, Turlock, California, Christian House.*

35

"No there's not because Jesus Christ said, 'no one comes to the Father except by me. I am the way, the truth, and the life.' "

Anonymous.

"I don't have any other choice but to believe in what Jesus said, because He is my authority, I have chosen Him to be my authority. And what He said is that, 'I am the way, the truth, and the life, no one comes to the Father but by me.' "

Shelley, San Mateo, California.

"They're all searching; that's one thing; and they've all found something in their religion. I know from instances and from experiences and from speaking with brothers who have been in other religions that they have no peace. Christ is a loving Savior and when you have Him in your heart you know as a creation that you have finally met your Creator."

Kathy, Texas, Resurrection City.

"If they don't believe in Jesus Christ and the Resurrection how can another religion be in with Christianity, or meet? Do you think that the Mormons and Hindus and Buddhists can ever find God? If they meet His conditions they can find God, meet the conditions that are the plan of salvation that is laid throughout the Bible. They should rethink their past life and get honest with themselves and realize what they are doing, how they are living, and see who they are living for, and anything that they put before God they should realize all that."

Sandra, Sunnyvale, California.

"Yea, they usually meet in the firing line, in not getting along with each other; being the point that Christianity is the acceptance of Jesus Christ as your personal Savior and other religions want to work their way into Heaven. There's no other way into Heaven but through Jesus Christ, so their meeting point is usually on grounds right there."

Amy, Girls' Teen Challenge of San Francisco.

"All the other religions won't get you to Heaven. Salvation through Jesus Christ is the only way to Heaven." *Carol, San Francisco, California.*

"I was in five/six different sects of, you know, all kinds of weird religions and I never experienced anything, you know. It was something I did. And only when at a point when I said, I can't do it—two days later I was introduced to the Lord Jesus, and only then have I seen the fruits; only then have I seen what God can do for somebody; only then is when I changed."

George, Jacksonville, Illinois.

Chapter 3

IS THERE A CHARISMATIC EXPLOSION?

If the Jesus Movement could be tagged with a denominational label, without doubt, it would have to fall under the category of Pentecostal—those who seek to be baptized with the Holy Spirit.

Of those interviewed for this book—a fair sampling of Jesus People—85 to 95 percent were associated in some way with the Pentecostals; they were exposed through their parents, or parent, or through some type of charismatic church.

What is the Holy Spirit?

"That's God. It's the Spirit. It's the contact we Christians have with God."   *Yoni, Greece.*

"It's the third person of the Godhead. There's God the Father, God the Son, and God the Holy Spirit. He's the one that Christ sent back to earth as the Comforter . . . an added power after you become a Christian. The Holy Spirit is our teacher. He's our protector and He leads us and guides us to truth. He's a personal person."   *Nancy, San Jose, California, Agape House.*

"The Holy Spirit is a part of God. He's the part that does the behind the scenes work, like influencing people and their thinking and He is their conscience."   *Sandra, Sunnyvale, California.*

"To me the Holy Spirit is the third person of the trinity. I have the Holy Spirit living within me."   *Gary, Redwood City, California.*

"God, Jesus Christ, and Heaven combined."
Robert, Portland, Oregon.

"The Holy Spirit is the spirit that Christ said was going to be left for us on the earth after He arose, and that way we would still be able to have fellowship with Christ through this—through the spirit."
Sally, Santa Cruz, California.

"God's spirit. I know He's with you all the time, and you walk hand-in-hand with Him all the time."
Chuck.

"It's something that helps you to do the will of God. It's something that when Jesus Christ went up, the Holy Spirit came down, and God is here, and It teaches you and stuff. It's Jesus in the form of a Spirit." *Debbie, San Jose, California, Maranatha House.*

"It s a comforter, teacher, and guide."
Sheila, Santa Barbara, California, Children of God.

"God represented to us. When we become a Christian the Holy Spirit comes to us and He helps us in our trials." *Kristal, San Mateo, California.*

"The Holy Spirit is the spirit who ascended on Jesus when He was baptized. It was witnessed by John. And ever since then, He let it be used for a teacher, and It's just the Spirit of God that teaches people."
Steve, Berkeley, California.

"It's something that shows me God's holiness. It's powerful. It's hard to believe It exists until It makes Itself real to you. It's indescribable."
Ken, Spokane, Washington.

"The Holy Spirit is the third part of the trinity. There is God the Father, God the Son, and God the Holy Ghost. The Holy Ghost baptizes you; you have the gift of speaking in tongues; you have one of the nine spiritual gifts. There is the gift of healing, the gift of

39

prophecy, the gift of speaking in tongues, the gift of interpretation of tongues, discernment of spirits."

Newton.

"What is the Holy Spirit? I'd say, 'Who is the Holy Spirit?' He's definitely a person in the trinity, the Godhead. I realize it like this; as God being a last name to a family of three, and there is the Father, Son, and the Holy Spirit. The Holy Spirit gives us power to witness, gives us understanding beyond our intelligence, wisdom beyond what we can understand, and gives us answers and ways of dealing with problems."

Amy, San Martin, California, Girls' Teen Challenge.

"The Holy Spirit can be grieved and vexed, blasphemed against. You can't blaspheme against an influence or a power, but He is a person."

Keith, Sunnyvale, California.

"Since Christ is not here now in physical form, then the Holy Spirit intercedes between man and God so the Holy Spirit is an interceder." *Anonymous.*

"The Holy Spirit is God, but the gift also is holy spirit. God is the Holy Spirit, capital 'H,' capital 'S,' and the holy spirit small 'h,' small 's,' is a gift that He gives to born-again believers."

Steve, Alameda, California, The Way.

"Strength, speaking in tongues, the baptism of the Holy Spirit, right? What is the Holy Spirit, period? The Spirit of God." *Carol.*

When did you receive the Holy Spirit?

"When I came into the world I received the Holy Spirit." *Neil, Detroit, Michigan.*

"I received the Holy Spirit the same time I became a disciple of Christ."

Cornelius, Dallas, Texas, Children of God.

"When I accepted Jesus."   *Micky, New Jersey.*

"Well, it was the minute that you confessed the Lord Jesus Christ as your Lord and Savior, you received the gift."
Steve, Alameda, California, The Way.

"I feel I received the Holy Spirit when I became a Christian. I felt Him knocking at my heart's door."
Gary, Redwood City, California.

"When I received Christ I received the Holy Spirit. I believe that when you receive Christ, the Holy Spirit enters you also; It grows as you mature as a Christian."   *Phil, San Mateo, California.*

"I got saved last December, 1970, and I received the Holy Spirit about a month later; but I still haven't grasped the whole concept of it. God is slowly showing me that this person, the Holy Spirit, what It is and what He can do, and how we have to give our whole lives every little thing to the Holy Spirit, so He can work with us."   *Anonymous.*

"About two months after I was saved."
Kathy, Resurrection City.

"Shortly after I was saved, I had a very distinct experience with the Holy Spirit. I don't know whether I count that as the day I received Him or not."
Christopher, San Francisco, California, House of Ebenezer.

"About a week after I asked Jesus into my heart; about eight months ago."
Ann, Los Gatos, California, Maranatha House.

"When I asked Jesus to fill me with it. I don't remember the date, but it has been a few years ago."
Ocem, Shyamea, Hawaii, Children of God.

"I received it about a year after I accepted the Lord."   *Anonymous.*

41

"If you mean speaking in tongues as receiving the Holy Spirit, I guess I was about ten."

Anonymous, Rochester, New York.

"My experience with receiving the Holy Spirit was kind of gradual, I didn't get 'slain in the spirit' or knocked to the floor or anything. I was down in the chapel and two or three of the people who were here that night decided to pray for me that night so that I might receive the gift of speaking in tongues. I was sitting there and they laid hands on me, praying that I would receive this. Specifically, they prayed that I would receive the gift of tongues. I did receive this gift. I'm really not too sure about the sequence of events. If after you're saved you receive the Holy Spirit, or if you receive the Holy Spirit when you get the gift of tongues."

Susan, Santa Cruz, California, D.A.P.C.

"I received it in a really small house, and before you know it I was speaking in different tongues, just like my whole mind was just—Wow! I don't know. It's beautiful . . . 'cause, just this different thing just really came over me. My eyes were opened to life."

Carol, San Francisco, California.

"The Bible says the Holy Spirit comes indwelling at the time of salvation, but the fullness of the Holy Spirit was another experience; that was the Baptism of the Holy Spirit. The Baptism was signified by speaking in tongues."

Daniel, Campbell, California, Maranatha House.

"After I was here for about three weeks, I was at this Charismatic Clinic. A week before I had tried to be baptized in the Holy Spirit; here the Lord showed me that I still had some hate in me. I wasn't forgiving, and there was unconfessed sin, and there were attitudes which weren't too Christian. I had to get rid of these, because if you're going to be baptized, you are going to have to be entirely clean and your soul has to be right with God. It took me all that week—and then some—to get all this purged out of me through prayer and fasting. At the Charismatic Clinic in Vallejo, in the middle of the service, I got this feeling that felt so good all over; so I felt better. And I was prophesying in tongues and speaking in tongues. It was just outta sight."   *Newton, San Francisco, California.*

"I don't know for sure if people can have the Holy Spirit, the gift, the power of God without speaking in tongues, because the Bible says it's evidence of the Holy Spirit—you must speak in tongues."
                    Nancy, San Jose, California, Agape Force.

"About three or four weeks after I was born again. I was in the middle of a whole bunch of people and they were praying for me and I was praying. First I was getting frustrated—I wouldn't talk in tongues, and I was going, 'Wow. What can I do?' And this woman that was there said, 'Don't get frustrated or have any doubts; just believe it and accept it.' So, I did, and all of a sudden I started praying in tongues. It was really far-out."

                    Gary, Menlo Park, California.

What's the difference between speaking in tongues and being filled with the spirit?

"Some people say there's no difference. I've heard both sides so much that I really don't know. I'd say you can be filled with the Spirit like it says when you become a Christian; God's Spirit is in you, so maybe you can say that that's filled with the Spirit, or there's a special time when you totally give up your own claims to your life, and let the Holy Spirit fill you then. Speaking in tongues is a definite time when your spiritual life grows to another step, but I can't say that it's synonymous with being filled with the Spirit."

Sandra, Sunnyvale, California.

"Every time I read in the Bible when someone has been filled with the Spirit, they always spoke in tongues, so I don't know. So I guess that was the best way. That is the way it happened."

Dan, Los Angeles, California, Agape Force.

"The Spirit gives you utterance and you speak in tongues. I don't feel that it is important who speaks in tongues, and who doesn't. I think that it is possible to be filled with the Spirit and not speak in tongues."

Syd, San Francisco, California, Song of Solomon House.

"I have never spoken in tongues, and I know that I was baptized in the Holy Spirit when I accepted the Lord Jesus Christ into my life as my personal Savior. I believe that tongues is a gift and that's all."

George, Jacksonville, Illinois, His House.

"Speaking in tongues is just a gift as another heavenly language in which you praise God. Being filled with the Spirit is just having God within you."

Karen, Reedley, California, Agape Force.

"When you accept Jesus Christ as your Lord and Savior, and believe God raised Him from the dead, you are filled with the Spirit. Whether you use it or not is up to you; according to what you know about how to use it, or whether you desire to use it. Speaking in tongues is the manifestation or operation of that gift."

Stephen, San Francisco, California, The Way.

"Speaking in tongues is just a gift of the Holy Spirit. I've been filled with the Spirit lots of times and I've never spoken in tongues."

Steve, Berkeley, California.

"You can be filled with the Spirit and speak in English. Matthew said that Jesus, full of the Spirit, was led up into the wilderness, for forty days to be tempted. And in the letters it talks about men speaking—full of the Holy Spirit."   *Bill, San Pablo.*

"Speaking in tongues is an unknown tongue; it's a gift of the Spirit. You don't have to speak in tongues to be filled with the Spirit and there are some who are not filled with the Holy Spirit who speak in tongues. The devil speaks in tongues and he sure isn't filled with the Holy Spirit."
         Maoch, Hayward, California, Children of God.

"The moment a person invites Jesus into his life, he becomes filled with the Spirit. Speaking in tongues is one manifestation of the Spirit. It is not necessary for salvation, and it isn't necessarily a sign of being filled with the Spirit. Speaking in tongues, in many cases, is a manifestation of the flesh. People get involved in emotionalism and it's a form of spiritual masturbation."   *Anonymous, Berkeley, California, C.W.L.F.*

"Well, if you're filled with the Holy Spirit, you're filled with light, whereas if you speak in tongues, it's been my experience that it's a psychic trip."
         Richard, Alameda, California, Home of Truth.

"Any Christian has the Spirit. Speaking in tongues is the symbol of the filling of the Spirit."
         Daniel, Campbell, California, Maranatha House.

"The evidence of being filled with the Holy Spirit is speaking in tongues. That's what the Bible says—as the Spirit gives you utterance. When I received the baptism of the Holy Spirit, that's how I know definitely that I had received it, because I did speak in an unknown tongue. When you first become a Christian, the Holy Spirit of Christ comes into your heart; but, then, there's another added gift; to be filled with the

Holy Spirit, and the evidence is speaking in tongues—
they both go together."

Nancy, San Jose, California, Agape Force.

"When you're filled with the Holy Spirit you have
these different gifts: prophecy is one of them; speaking in tongues is one of the gifts. Actually, they're the
same thing, because when you speak in tongues you're
filled with the Holy Spirit. Speaking in tongues is one
of the manifestations of the Holy Spirit."

Ronald, San Francisco, California.

"Speaking in tongues, I think, is just a special gift
from God; just like prophecy or the ability to preach;
or just the ability to make friends and help others.
You can be filled—in all of these things; you're filled
with the Spirit, and they're all gifts of the Holy
Spirit." *Alicia.*

"In my opinion, you are not filled with the Spirit
unless you speak in tongues."

Gary, Menlo Park, California.

"The speaking in tongues, the way I've had it
described to me, is that it is just a result of being
filled with the Spirit."

Kathy, Berkeley, California, Resurrection City.

"When you are filled with the Holy Ghost, you
speak in tongues. Speaking in tongues isn't the Holy
Ghost; tongues is a sign of being filled with the Holy
Ghost."

Anonymous, Sunnyvale, California.

"All I can say is when I received Jesus, I was filled
with love, joy and happiness; and when I received the
Holy Ghost I spoke in tongues, and I was in a higher
state of ecstasy than I had ever had before; that's all I
can tell you."

Steve, Turlock, California, Christian House.

"I think that when you're baptized in the Holy Spirit, you speak in tongues; but when you ask the Lord into your heart, you have part of His Spirit."
Debbie, Campbell, California, Maranatha House.

"They are inseparable. You can't speak in tongues unless you've been baptized in the Holy Spirit. It's a by-product. When you're baptized with water, you have a by-product, you get wet. Same thing with tongues—it's just a by-product. It's a sign that you've been baptized with the Holy Ghost."
Newton, San Francisco, California.

"Speaking in tongues is a manifestation of the Baptism of the Holy Spirit. You need neither one to be saved; but, take a dinner table—when the salt and pepper is on the table, the food is a lot better, and that is kind of what tongues is—it sweetens up everything."
Martin, Campbell, California, House of Uttering.

Have you sought to speak in tongues?

"I asked the Lord to give it to me, and—praise God!" *Steve, Thornton, California, Christian House.*

"When I was younger I sought it, and finally I did and I still do." *Sandra, Sunnyvale, California.*

"Yea, I sought and got my prayers answered."
Ken, Spokane, Washington, Maranatha House.

"Yes, I speak in tongues."
Kathy, Sunnyvale, California, Maranatha House.

"Yes, because the Bible says that it is from God, and a lot of my friends have had it, and it really edifies them, and it gave them a relationship with the Lord that they never had."
Debbie, Massachusetts, Maranatha House.

47

"Yes I have. I did it for special reasons because I wanted to really get in fellowship with God."

Anonymous.

"Yeah. I speak in tongues every day. It's refreshing and I can communicate with God as long as I want to. It's like the Spirit of God controls my tongue. This language is talking with men, but talking in tongues is to talk to God with."

Gary, Menlo Park, California.

"For three days, I sought to speak in tongues, or more perfectly, to know this baptism of the Holy Spirit, because I knew something was lacking in my life. I did seek to speak in tongues . . . I thought it was a valid thing."

C. G., Mill Valley, California, Ivy House.

"No, and I believe that if the Lord wants me to, He will. I can't do anything. I want to please the Lord, and the only thing I seek is to do the Lord's will, not my will. And the Lord's will be done, not my will be done. And I feel, I see a lot of people doing non-scriptural things with tongues, and I believe in the Bible 100%; and anything unscriptural I don't believe in." *George, Jacksonville, Illinois, His House.*

"No, I don't speak in tongues." *Anonymous.*

"Speaking in tongues can be of the Spirit, or of your own creation. If it's of the Spirit, your voice becomes resonant, mellow, deeper and you almost cannot say a lie. You cannot tell a lie if the Spirit is speaking through you. It's just like in Revelation; His voice was like many waters." *Byron, Miami, Florida.*

". . . when I was a young Christian and other people tried to get me to speak in tongues letting my jaw always flap and making me make all kinds of funny sounds and it became very apparent to me that if God wanted me to speak in tongues, I would speak in tongues, without doing all these artificial things."

Anonymous.

"At one time I did seek to 'speak in tongues' but too often it was just an emotional build-up thing where I mumbled a bunch of words that I never knew what they meant or anything like that, and Paul says that God is not the author of confusion."

Bob, El Cajon, California.

"Yes, when I first became a Christian the people that I was with told me that you had to do it. So I prayed that I could do it, and I went as far as copying off them so they would think that I had the gift."

Steve, Berkeley, California.

"I can speak in tongues now—it's a gift of God. It's not a thing that you—you seek to receive it; you ask God to give it to you, according to Luke 11; you ask God, and He gives it to you. Just another tool, you see, for winning souls."

Cornelius, Hayward, California, Children of God.

"No. I don't think it's necessary and I think that speaking in tongues was assigned to the Jews because they were always looking for a sign. I think it was assigned to show them that Christ had come, and I don't think I need it."

Alicia.

"I think it sort of happened all by itself. Every time it happened it sort of comes out by itself. I feel something welling up inside me and all of a sudden I'm speaking in tongues."

Anonymous.

"When I first met the family, I didn't want to speak in tongues because the church told me it was wrong; that it split the church. And anything of God would not split the church. I was really afraid of it, and I thought they were all wrong. I heard other people speaking in tongues. It got to a point where I wanted to tell Jesus how much I loved Him, and just praise Him. I only had so much in my vocabulary to say; and I loved Him so much more than my vocabulary would ever say. And I wanted to speak in tongues, and that's why I received it. I probably received it before, but I would never accept it, until I actually wanted to tell God how much I loved Him and I came down speaking in tongues and letting the Spirit speak through me, to God, telling Him the things I couldn't express."

Sheila, Santa Barbara, California, Children of God.

"I do speak in tongues. I didn't really seek, but 'when I wanted it, I just asked for it and got it.' "

Michelle, Redwood City, California, House of Manna.

"No, I haven't because my church frowns on it so much. Lots of my friends have, and they have had very negative things about it so I just have never tried it."

Kristal, San Mateo, California.

"There are a lot of believers that speak in tongues that aren't filled with the Holy Spirit. The Scripture says that when they were filled with the Holy Spirit they spoke in other tongues as the Spirit gave utterance. I think that there is a lot of born-again Christians that speak in tongues. I know personally from my life, that I can speak in tongues and not be in communion with God. Then there is actually when the Spirit is speaking out too, where He actually takes control of your tongue. I never sought to speak in tongues. I sought to be filled with the Holy Spirit and after being filled with the Holy Spirit, I spoke in tongues."

Anonymous, Texas.

"Yes, I speak in tongues every day. Every hour I speak in tongues; it really builds me up. It gives me wisdom in a lot of areas. I can't really explain how it does, but it just does."

Martin, Campbell, California, House of Uttering.

"Yes, when I first received it, I was thinking, 'Did God give this to me or what is this?' There was a lot of differences in my opinion about it and I even stopped speaking in tongues because I was afraid that it was not of the Lord, but just through my walk with God more and more, I felt a desire to go forth in it and really use it and Christ through the Word of God, revealed to me that it was from Him and that it was a gift to all of His children. It was to bring me closer to Him and so I went forth in it . . . it's a new language that you continue to practice."

Kathy, Texas, Resurrection City.

Have you ever had a dream or prophecy come true?

"I've had lots of prophecies come true. I don't know who prophesied them but I prayed for them. I've had dreams come true and I know they came from God, and I know the reason I'm here right now in an apartment I'm not paying for, and I'm in a ministry for Christ. I'm in a Santa Clara school—I never should have been in—it is directly a result of God."

Mark, Portland, Oregon.

"I've had both come true. I really think it came from God."

Ken, Spokane, Washington, Maranatha House.

"Yes, I have, and I think it came from God because I feel that God wanted me to have to do a certain thing because He had a certain reason for me to do it, you know, like explaining something to another person— you know, explaining about God."

Richard, Turlock, California.

"Yes. I have. (from God?) Absolutely. I can't go into details but the Lord revealed to me the woman I

51

was going to marry and how I was going to marry her and what I was going to say to her and it all took place exactly."

Anonymous, Berkeley, California, Christian World Liberation Front.

"I've had a few dreams that were from God. They all came true in a sense. Some of them are future concerning my life."

Rich, Campbell, California, Maranatha House.

"All my life. I've dreamed a dream of being with the Lord, being with God's perfect will; and it came true. I met the Children of God. The testimony of Jesus is the spirit of prophecy. (Rev. 19: 10) And we are living prophecy right now. It says in Isaiah 11: 11 that 'it shall come to pass in that day that the Lord shall send His hand a second time to recover the remnant of his people, from the four quarters of the earth.' And that's what God is doing . . . we're living Bible prophecy right now."

Cornelius, Dallas, Texas, Children of God.

"Yes. I definitely had a dream of prophecy, and I believe that it was from God, because I was administering salvation to a man in my dream, and he got saved, and in reality I did administer salvation to this man, and he did get saved."

Kyle, Berkeley, California, Resurrection City.

"I've had a lot of dreams that Jesus was in—it's not like they could come true—they teach me something."

Steve, Berkeley, California.

"Yes, I had a dream come true, not of my own dream but I had a dream of another person that came true, but I didn't tell that person; like I didn't prophesy that dream. After it came true I told that person that I had had a dream about a month ago about this." *Sandra, Sunnyvale, California.*

"Yeah. I've had 3 dreams come true. Yes. Because I was psychic for 3 days and those 3 nights I dreamed dreams that came true the next day."

Byron, Miami, Florida.

"When we first moved into this house and not more than a week later I had a dream that we wouldn't be in this house very long. I didn't say anything to anybody. I didn't think too much of it. I did tell our leader about it though. I was just kidding around because I didn't know if it was for real or not, but we went home for Thanksgiving and I found out that this house was sold. We have to move out. We have to be out by the 10th of January. It hasn't come true yet altogether. The Lord could just step right in and just have somebody have the money so we can buy this house."

Nancy, San Jose, California, Agape House.

Do you think a person can be miraculously healed?

"I believe that every person that is baptized in the Holy Spirit has all the gifts of the Spirit. But if you mean gifts that are operating: tongues, sometimes interpretation of tongues, prophecy, and I just started with healing." *Anonymous.*

"Jesus left the earth and He said He'd send a Comforter to enable us to do the things He had done and to build His Kingdom here on earth. The Holy Spirit gives me strength. It leads me and It guides me. I can't preach to people or tell about Jesus or if I'm called upon to heal somebody, I can't do anything unless the Holy Spirit has to come through me to do that." *Rich, Campbell, California, Maranatha House.*

"I was healed. It's a long story but how I was healed was that Jesus touched me and healed me. In 1961, I

53

shot some heroin that had some strychnine in it. This caused permanent nerve damage. Then I got Parkinson's disease. And I was eating vitamins and reds and everything else to try to keep calm. But it was of no effect. In 1965 I got my head bashed in with a hammer which made me into an epileptic and I would have seizures 2 or 3 times a day unless I would keep myself doped up with phenobarbital. In 1967 I got thrown out of a freight train and my back got torn up and I had to wear a back brace the rest of my life. My back muscles had atrophied and I didn't have any. I had bleeding ulcers; I had been on ulcer medicine for over two years and my right ankle was smashed. It had a bone protruding. In 2 seconds flat Jesus touched me and healed the whole mess. [Was this when you received Christ?] Yes, this happened here at Teen Challenge at one of our Night of Miracles Rally."

Newton, San Francisco, California.

Chapter 4

IS LOVE WHERE IT'S AT?

What the Jesus People have to say about love may surprise some readers. Their definitions of love vary from feelings of friendliness to intense self-denial.

Most Jesus People agreed that sex is reserved for the bonds of marriage. They say premarital sex fulfills lust. While some Jesus People grant the privileges of premarital sex to non-Christians, they oppose the same conduct for Christians.

How do you define love?

"Love is not a feeling. I had many girls before I met the Lord. Even then to show my love, I denied myself. That's real love. It's not a feeling. I share what I have with her. Usually the best thing is the Word of God, the wisdom of God; something that will help her soul."
Cornelius, Hayward, Children of God.

"I believe that the love is completely opposite from the love of the world between man and a woman. It starts in the spirit and then it goes into the soulish realm and then into the physical realm."
Kathy, Berkeley, California, Resurrection City.

"You can find the answer in I Corinthians the Thirteenth Chapter—what real love is, I think, that's how you should express yourself." *Chuck.*

"Some men treat their friends a lot better than they do their wives. She should be your friend. Someone you can share things with and have a good relationship with. Something that is pure and wholesome."

Bob, El Cajon, California.

"You should express yourself with respect toward a girl that you love. You should be completely, wholeheartedly honest with yourself; and know that you really love that girl for who she is, and what she is."

C. G., Mill Valley, California, Ivy House.

How does love develop?

"When you really like a girl, I feel the relationship should be one that depends on the Lord Jesus Christ, both parties trusting Him." *Howard, Alameda.*

How do you express love?

"How to express love to a girl? That's a good question. Because I love a girl, and I haven't done a thing." *Keith, Sunnyvale, California.*

"Take her out, do little things for her, share the Word with her. Definitely not premarital sex, because that is not doing her much of a favor."

Phil, San Mateo, California

"And I think the neatest way I can express my love for her is not just beating her over the head with Scripture, but by being able to show her I love her just by helping around the house and by making myself available. Show her that I always have enough time to sit down and that she's really number one."

Mark, Portland, Oregon.

"If I found out I loved him, I'd try to treat him like Jesus, with a lot of respect."

Debbie, Campbell, California, Maranatha House.

"I express my love to her with kisses. I kind of dig hugging a lot, holding hands, really personal touch."

Anonymous.

"If I loved a girl, I would make sure she was a Christian. If she wasn't a Christian, I'd get her saved. That's the best thing I can do for anybody."

Newton, San Francisco, California.

"I would find out the things she likes, like she might like a ring, or picture, or something like that, or a certain gift, or perfume or something that is special to her." *Richard, Turlock, California, Rapping Post.*

"I'll have to be general and say in whatever way is edifying and glorifying to the Lord."

Steve, Mountain View, California.

Do you feel premarital sex is right, or not right?

"Sex outside of marriage is definitely forbidden, and any other kind of foreplay is defrauding."

Anonymous.

"I can't even make-out with a chick because in my mind I keep thinking all kinds of thoughts and it just tears me down spiritually, and pretty soon it will start getting to her. I'm not anti-sexual either, because I'm going to get married someday and I'm going to enjoy sex probably as much as anyone who has had it with 100 different partners. It's going to be with one person and it's going to be something fantastic."

Bob, El Cajon, California.

"I used to dig it but I know it's the false truth of the world. And you see so many mothers walking around with kids, without fathers. You can look and see that V.D. is an epidemic and it's just not right-on, it never was." *Gary, San Francisco, California.*

"I feel you really shouldn't get too physical because you aren't married. You know. And if something comes along you might not be able to support both of them." *Richard, Turlock, California, Rapping Post.*

"I've never gone to bed with a chick since I've become a Christian two and one half years ago, just because I don't want to hurt anybody, and I know what it can do to a person inside to do that." *Bob, El Cajon, California.*

"There's the way of courting a woman I think the Bible states. I don't think we should get into lust; it's not where it's at. It blinds you to the real truth." *Morry.*

"Kiss, hug—you have to look at the Lord, but as far as I'm concerned, I don't need to get any closer than that until we're married, because the love that God gives us is enough." *Steve, Turlock, California, The Christian House.*

"Well, the Word of God, of course, tells us that getting carried away in the flesh before marriage isn't too cool, and the Lord would really convict you if you were open to the Spirit—if you were kind of getting carried away." *Troy, Turlock, California, Christian House.*

"That's totally against God and what it says in Scripture. It's something that has been coming out in the last century or so. I believe that the Devil has a hand, a rise in the intellectuality and everybody's beginning to rationalize. It should have no place in you. It's something that will ruin your life."

Rick, Campbell, California, Maranatha House.

"Premarital sex is an abomination in the eyes of God, because there's one man for every woman, and one woman for every man."

C. G., Mill Valley, California, Ivy House.

"It says in the Scriptures that a woman never even left her home and never left her virginity until after she joined the man."

Ann, Campbell, California, Maranatha House.

"I don't see anything wrong with it, although the Ten Commandments say 'thou shalt not commit adultery.' That is the same thing as fornication without being married. I've broken the Ten Commandments so often I don't really know what's right anymore."

Byron.

"It depends on what kind of girl she is . . . if she was a Christian girl or if she's not, and it depends on the situation." Morry.

"If you feel that it really deepens your relationship with Christ, and you feel that Christ would not be harmed about it, you should go ahead."

Rock, Richmond, California, Christian House.

"I think for Christians it's wrong. I think for a heathen, if it feels good, and they want to do it; fine."

Bill, San Pablo, California.

How far should you go?

"As a sister, you should love her, cherish her, and keep your hands off her."

Anonymous, Berkeley, California, C.W.L.F.

"I believe the Bible says not to do anything to cause desires that you can't fill. I think that's where you draw the line—don't do anything that would make you want to neck."

Teresa, Redwood City, California, The Way Inn.

"Out of marriage you should be extremely careful. I don't know of any Scripture that says you can't kiss. But when you know how to ride a bicycle, you hate to go back to a trike." Anonymous.

"The Bible states very clearly on the matter. I Corinthians 7: 1 says that it is not good to touch a woman. It's not good for a man because it would be tempting his flesh. I would say that even before you kiss a woman you should know that she's the one you're going to marry. If you wanted to go on the basis of how physical you should get, you should have a set date of marriage before you'd even kiss her."

Daniel, Campbell, California, Maranatha House.

"Well I rub my girlfriend's back and she rubs mine; but physical comes later, spiritual comes first."

Nick, Turlock, California, Leader at His House.

"You wouldn't have to try to express yourself. You should go as far as she lets you." Byron.

Should a Christian feel free to use contraceptives?

"I'm not married and I don't have sex. That's my birth control."

George, Turlock, California, His House.

"I don't think that there is anything wrong with it, mostly because some women that I know—that I just really respect—and who I know are really close to the Lord use birth control."

Debbie, Campbell, California, Maranatha House.

"I can't say that they should abstain, because I'd be a hypocrite because when I get married, I plan to use them." *Sandra.*

"I couldn't say. I'm not married, so I don't know what I'd do."
Kathy, Berkeley, California, Resurrection City.

"Some of our girls didn't believe in contraceptives, and they were having one baby and BANG another baby. The Pill is really a logical thing to use, because it doesn't mean you can't have kids anymore, but you can just take care of it for awhile."
Sally, Santa Cruz, California, Drug Abuse Preventative Center.

"I think there are too many people in the world now and if a child is going to be born that isn't loved—that doesn't make sense—so I think that contraceptives are a good idea." *Kristal.*

"It is becoming a serious problem with over-population. There are so many families having too many kids because maybe they are forbidden to use birth control pills." *Mildred.*

"Right now we're having a real problem with the population. If you have a whole bunch of kids, you can't care for them or you can't love them, you really can't care for them."
Alicia.

"I believe that if God wants you to have children, you will have children; if God doesn't want you to have children, you won't. I think contraceptives are an abomination."
C. G., Mill Valley, California, Ivy House.

"Personally, I would not use contraceptives, because in the beginning when God spoke, let man multiply

61

and replenish the earth, nowhere did he say that man should control birth or anything like that."

Daniel, Campbell, California, Maranatha House.

"You want to know the best contraceptive? It's God. It says in the Bible, He can close up a woman's womb, and she can't bear."

Eric, San Mateo, California, Brothers House.

"I feel that this is something that has to be between the couple and the Lord. I believe the Pill is like a drug itself with too many side effects, and it can be very dangerous." *Doug.*

"For Christians there shouldn't be any messing around at all. For secular people, contraceptives could be the lesser of two evils. People going through the engagement period of sexual activity, it could be the wisest thing to use these, so they wouldn't bring misery upon a child." *Tim.*

"I think it's up to the individual and he should seek the Lord. I think it's good to have a lot of kids though from what the Scriptures say. Psalm 128 states that happy is the man who has a whole bunch of them."

Morry.

What is the marriage relationship?

"One thing that the Lord desires to show is that the marriage relationship is symbolic of a relationship with Christ and the Church." *Howard.*

"It says in I Corinthians that Christ is the head of the Church, and that man is the head of the woman. A woman is supposed to be submissive to her husband; a woman was made for the man, and the woman was of the man. They are both not independent, but the woman is supposed to be subject to her husband."

Cornelius, Hayward, Children of God.

"Marriage and that type of love is something that God will put in both their hearts and they'll find the same interests. With God, we should start with the spiritual, just being around a sister and studying with her and going to meetings with her, and then as you continue to move on, you'll see that perhaps God is moving you together, and then you can move on to praying together, and the final thing will culminate in the physical when it gets up to the hand-holding and the kissing; and when you get married, the sexual. The way the world goes, they have it reversed."

Rick, Campbell, California, Maranatha House.

"The Bible says greater love than this hath no man, that he lay down his life for his friends. If I really love somebody, I'm going to lay down my life for them. Not just physically, but everyday by putting them above me, above my needs, above my wants. You see, I'm going to put them first, do whatever I can to help them."

Shelia, Hayward, California, Children of God.

Should a Christian have only one wife?

"I believe one wife is about all anyone can handle."
Rekum, Hayward.

"If your attention is divided with so many women, you really can't give that much love to the Lord, and it really shows that you're not really getting all your needs fulfilled in one person."   *Mickie.*

"I think that all Christians should have one wife. You cannot serve two masters."   *Anonymous.*

"I haven't read up on Abraham or anything, but I know that gluttony is a sin and if you have too many wives, then that is gluttony."

Robert, Haight-Ashbury.

63

"I think that the marriage relationship is the direct expression of the relationship of Christ with His church. It's a symbol. The man is to the wife as Christ is to the church, and Christ doesn't have many churches, He has one Church."

Christopher, San Francisco, California, Ebenezer House.

Chapter 5

DROP OUT? OR JUMP IN?

What happens when one of these new converts becomes a Christian? Does he drop out of society? Generally speaking the Jesus Movement revolves around the drug counter-culture of ex-drug, society dropouts. Their old life-style and thoughts come into direct confrontation with structure presented from a Biblical standpoint.

They drop their old life-style immediately, not because of lack of devotion to ideals, but because their old system offered no workable rationale to the lofty ideals. Retaining these ideals (humanitarian), they jump into a new society where a new approach to those ideals can manifest itself.

In this chapter the points of discussion revolve around their old style "down with society"; but they move toward the incorporation of their new ideal—"Jesus is the answer."

Direct political stances will show their dilemma; contradictions abound; and yet, their goal stands —a NEW SOCIETY UNDER GOD.

What is society?

"One thing that many people believe; I know, I believed it for a while, that God created the world and society which is a false belief. God did not create the society; man created the society. Therefore; the society is bad."   *Anonymous.*

"Society is made up of people, and it's got hierarchies in it, and in our society we elect to have authority over us. In other societies, people are put in authority or take authority. There's power structure and within it there's laws. There is rules, regulations with some kind of acknowledgement of their need for one another."   *Shelley, San Mateo, California.*

"Society is the established order of events: it's the set pattern of how people do things."
Cornelius, Dallas, Texas, Children of God.

"I think when you became a Christian you're supposed to be out of the world. Society is what everybody does. Society has rules of its own, and social standards, and if it's not according to the Bible, then it shouldn't be done."
Nancy, Reedley, California, Agape Force.

"Society defined is: grasping, clinging, trying to take, making the dollar their God. I think that it is basically just a similar interest in trying to achieve some sort of equality and peace I guess."
Ann, Los Gatos, California, Maranatha House.

What's wrong with our society?

"Like all societies we've suffered from being separated from God and not doing His will as a corporate whole. And I think the results are being seen."
Steve, Mountain View, California.

"I feel that our society, not only our society but the society of the world, is controlled by the Prince of this world."   *Amy, San Martin, California.*

"When a nation forgets God, then God forgets the nation. And that's why America and all other nations are having problems now."
                 Cornelius, Dallas, Texas, Children of God.

"I think the problem isn't the society, or isn't capitalists, or isn't communists, or isn't socialists, but it's the people. The people make the society. The people set up the system, and I think we try to deal with just the symptom of the problem if we try to remove capitalism and replace it with something else."   *Mark, Portland, Oregon.*

"I'm for theocracy. God-controlled, God-dictatorship, Christ. Before I was a Christian, I was completely left. But I found even in the left, there's no dedication. They all play games."   *Cornelius, Dallas, Texas.*

"Christians should be the leaders of society. That's the only way society is going to make it and stay together until the Rapture happens."
                 Newton, San Francisco, California.

"I believe that any government or any social structure can't work in the first place outside of God. Capitalism is every man for himself, competing, and working against every other man. That's not God in the first place. That'll never work. That builds on each man's selfishness, each man's pride, to get ahead of the other guy. Communism is everyone sharing everything they have, with someone on top to distribute what's there. That's God. Everyone sharing and loving each other. But without God, like I said it won't work, because it's every man working against every other man."   *C. G., Mill Valley, Ivy House.*

"It is almost getting like Sodom and Gomorrah."
Dan, Los Angeles, California.

"I think our society, like the society before, and the society before that, are still full of sin. It's sick, always has been and always will be. And the only thing that will change it is a turning back to God."
Nick, Turlock, California.

"I think the government should repent and turn to God." *Cornelius, Dallas, Texas, Children of God.*

"I think if Christians weren't in this society that society would collapse; the whole order of things would just die out and dissolve, and there would be complete disorder. It says in the Bible that Christians are the salt of the earth and the salt is the savor to the earth and it would be just a plain . . . blah."
Sandra, Sunnyvale, California.

Should a Christian drop out?

"Definitely; all Christians should drop out. If you read the Bible, you would see that all Christians drop out. Jesus said, 'Repent for the Kingdom of Heaven is at hand.' Repent is from the Greek word *metanoia,* meaning revolution. To turn around, U-turn. When a Christian, a real Christian, meets the Lord, really meets Jesus Christ, he makes a U-turn, a revolution. He turns around from the established order and goes the other direction. That's what Christianity means."
Cornelius, Dallas, Texas, Children of God.

"I'm not interested in politics myself. It's the only way you can save your material world (if you want to control the material world)."
Byron, Miami, The Vega Hut.

"If you get involved in local affairs, you can't get involved in the affairs Jesus wants you to. He said go out to the highways and the byways and bring them in. You can't do it if you're saying, 'Vote for muck-a-de-muck.' Instead you should be saying, 'Praise the Lord.' "   *Newton, San Francisco, California.*

"I don't think that a Christian really has that kind of time to spend getting involved in man's government, because our whole reason for being here on this earth is to preach God's Word, to warn the people."
    Sheila, Santa Barbara, California, Children of God.

"Political actions are not part of the Christian's walk. We talk about God; we talk about the Bible, and what God is going to be doing from the Bible. And you don't have time for politics."
    Maoch, Hayward, California, Children of God.

"We are society. Every person is society. I can't understand why people talk about dropping out of society, because we are society—every person. If we're in one society or another society—we're going to be in society. We're going to be a hippie, or a straight, or a greaser, or a freak—you're in society whether you want to be or not."
    George, Jacksonville, Illinois, His House.

"I think that instead of pulling ourselves out of it we should put ourselves into it and shine as walking right with God that we may be examples."
    Ken, Spokane, Washington, Maranatha House.

"I believe that if the Senate and Congress and politicians were to commit their lives to Christ, our government would be a better government."
    Chuck, Mississippi.

"I think we should drop out of sin, and we won't need to drop out of society."
    Mike, Salt Lake City, Utah.

"I don't think you should actually drop out of the system; you should kind of stay in it, in a way. We should be connected with it, but not going on Satan's bandwagon." *Ronald, San Francisco, California.*

"No; I think Christ never gave a command to drop out of anything. I think He said, 'Do the best you can with what is given to you,' and nothing is given to a man unless it is given by God; and I think that that clearly states what we're supposed to do as Christians." *Kyle, Berkeley, California, Resurrection City.*

"I'd say we're in the society we live in, and we ought to communicate with the people in it."
Howard, Alameda, California.

"If we drop out like the monks, we're not doing anything and God can't use us. In a sense we're selfish—we're stealing from society."
Rick, Campbell, California, Maranatha House.

"I feel that a Christian should be involved in political action in the way of voting, being involved in military service, and being against whatever is against God. I don't think they have to be out parading with signs, or chasing around in riots, or whatever."
Amy, San Martin, California, Girls' Teen Challenge.

"I think that Christians really have it together a lot better than most people. We can really see it [the nation] falling apart around us. I think if the Christians get busy and take some action, then maybe it can stay together a little longer."
Alicia, San Francisco, California.

"I think that it is really important for Christians to be involved in the government and stuff, because it says in the Bible that the people who rule over us are ordained by God. I think that it is really important that we have Christian people ruling our country

because that's an even better chance for the Gospel to be spread. If there are Christians making the laws and stuff, then it is going to be a better place to live."
Debbie, Massachusetts, Maranatha House.

"I think it's up to the individual. I think the best thing to do would be to pray for your leaders if you want to get involved, that God would guide them and give us intelligent and wise leaders. I don't think an anti-war rally is going to stop wars. In order to really change things, you have to go through the right channels." *Morry, Carmel, California.*

How do you feel about civil rights?

"I believe it was the Apostle Paul who said, 'If you were free when you were converted, then stay free, and if you were a slave when you were converted, then stay a slave.' Slavery was an accepted practice in those days. It wasn't a sin in the apostles' days, and I don't believe it's a sin now." *Bill, San Pablo, California.*

"The whites have oppressed the blacks; the blacks have oppressed the whites. The yellows have oppressed the whites; the whites have oppressed the yellows. Everybody has oppressed everybody else."
Maoch, Hayward, California, Children of God.

"I feel that all of us are prejudiced in one way or another, and it would be a lie if I said I wasn't prejudiced in one form or another. I know that the Lord is cleansing my prejudice."
Kyle, Berkeley, California, Resurrection City.

"We all have equal rights. Christian rights are under God, and until everyone becomes a Christian and can see the truth, no one's gonna have any rights." *Steve, Thornton, California, Christian House.*

71

"Civil rights? I don't even know what that means. I used to try to find out what it meant. But you see, all men are wicked; and there will never be civil rights until Christ comes into a man's life."

Cornelius, Dallas, Texas, Children of God.

"I've got my Jesus and that's my civil rights, right there. I've got my focus. Civil rights, like Women's Lib, comes from sin." *Shelley, San Mateo, California.*

"All human beings have been done wrong by each other. We just hate each other so much. The Lord doesn't really want us to get out there and get our rights for ourselves. I think we should leave it up to the Lord. As Christians, we should not worry about our own rights, but worry about helping other people." *Steve, Mountain View, California.*

"I think civil rights is part of truth itself, and whether it is associated with God's truth, I think that the truth that Martin Luther King was telling about is all a part of the truth that comes from God."

John, El Cajon, California.

"I think that God, with His mercy and love, freed the people, and freed the blacks. And I think that civil rights is a very valid movement, because I think it's a spiritual movement, as well as physical."

Kyle, Berkeley, California, Resurrection City.

Do you believe in war in general?

"I think if you are going to fight a war the two presidents, the president of each country, should fight. If they have to be killed, just let them kill each other so that millions of other people wouldn't have to be killed." *Richard, Turlock, California.*

"I don't feel that any war is right. I don't think that there is a moral or just war." *Chuck, Mississippi.*

72

"According to our capitalist system, our oppressive system, you've got to have a way to keep the economy. It's inspired by Satan, and it's just another means of making money for society. It says, 'From what comes wars and what causes fightings among you? Is it not your passions that are at war in your members?' You see, wars they are from man's evil heart. They are inspired by Satan, because they don't have the love of God." *Cornelius, Dallas, Texas, Children of God.*

"To prevent wars we should seek the Lord and ask what He wants for our life."
Steve, Mountain View, California.

"Any war is an abomination in the eyes of God. We should have no man kill any other man for any reason. Jesus was the perfect example of prejudice, of oppression, of persecution. He had everything going against Him that any man ever did. He didn't lift one finger or say one word to defend himself, but rather laid down His life." *C. G., Mill Valley, Ivy House.*

"It's wrong. It's going against the teachings of God. It just shows what man will do by his nature."
Steve, Berkeley, California.

What do you think about the draft?

"A Christian is serving God with all of his heart, and his will is in the hands of God, and if a draft notice comes and he is to go into the service, then the truth of the matter is that God wants him in the service, and he should go."
Martin, Campbell, California, House of Uttering.

"If the government told me to go to war, I would because He told me to obey that government and if I felt like I didn't want to go to war, if I felt that it was wrong, I tell Him, 'I don't feel this is right. Maybe You

73

don't want me to go. You can change their minds so
that I don't have to go.'"

Shauna, Fresno, California, Agape Force.

"If I were drafted, would I go? I have been drafted
and I'm going to refute it because I'm serving God,
even if I go to jail."

Rekum, Santa Barbara, California, Leader in the Chil-
dren of God.

"A Christian should resist anything that has to do
with war. God has nothing to do with war. I believe a
Christian can be in the army for only one purpose, and
that is to witness to the other people in the army. A
Christian can never carry a gun, and I believe that few
Christians can even be in the army."

C. G., Mill Valley, California, Ivy House.

"I think in some cases there are people that really,
really believe that it is exactly against God's commandments. So they are C.O.'s, and they'll be willing
to go to jail. And if they really and truly believe that
way, then OK. I really don't know that much about it.

Shauna, Fresno, California, Agape Force.

"It's not of God. I think it's prophesied in the Bible;
it's predicted. I don't think it's God's will at all. My
inner man says to rebel against the draft, to rebel
against going over there. It's partial fear and partial
that it's not God's will to kill, but God may call me to
help heal or to help save."

Ken, Spokane, Washington, Maranatha House.

Do you think the Women's Lib gals are right on?

"They're teed off because they're just a rib. I
would be too if that's what I was called."

Byron, Miami, Florida.

"Well, I feel that there's a validity in the women's lib, because women in this society right now have been oppressed. But I think the ultimate freedom a woman could find would be the freedom of the spirit in Jesus." *Kyle, Berkeley, California, Resurrection City.*

"They're to submit to men; they're for men. Man was lonely, and she was given to him. Woman was taken out of man to serve man. As Christ is the head of the church, man is the head of woman. I'm not much for women's lib."
George, Jacksonville, Illinois, His House.

"Women's lib is sin. I think a lot of people treat women unjustly, unrightly. The Bible says for wives to be subject to their husbands, but on the other hand, it says for the husbands to cherish their wives. And if a husband was actually doing his part in keeping up the love of God in that relationship, then the woman wouldn't feel like she was getting the rotten end of the deal."
Ken, Spokane, Washington, Maranatha House.

"I think women's lib is a manifestation of Satan. It's a working of fear; fear of not being able to cope in what society calls a man's society. Fear of not being able to get their just dues and wanting things better for themselves." *Shelley, San Mateo, California.*

"Men should be in authority over women in the marriage situation, and in church situations, and whatever situations there are, simply because God has laid it out that way, and the Bible has laid it out that way." *C. G., Mill Valley, Ivy House.*

"Women's lib is a tragic thing, because usually I find these women have had a very unpleasant experience with a man in their lives; with a boyfriend, or a Father, or something in which they have been used

75

and mistreated. If we had men of God who would look to woman in her God-given role, then the women wouldn't be complaining, because there would be real love relationships going on. With the man leading and directing, and the woman inspiring. I know several Christian couples where the women have taken this role as an inspiration, a helpmate, and they are the most happy and contented women that I have seen around."

John, Whittier, California, Agape Force.

"I don't think that women are inferior in intelligence. Perhaps some men think that women are inferior, and behave accordingly, but I think that the Bible displays what the man's role and what the women's role is. It is not a matter of equality, of one being superior, or not. It is just a matter of harmony, and how God wants us to respond to each other."

Chuck, Mississippi.

"I think that a woman is a weaker vessel. The Bible says she's got different qualities than a man does. I think that women should be in the home, and the man should be the one who's the head of the house. And the woman, if she can, should try to go along with her husband as much as she can, and respect Him."

Morry, Carmel, California.

Chapter 6

ARE MY PARENTS REALLY NECESSARY?

You might be a parent of one of the Jesus People, or you might be aware of problems between parents and youth who are involved in this Movement.

If so, you may already know how many parents feel toward the youth. In this chapter, you will search out the attitudes of the Jesus People toward parents.

The comments you find in the chapter will relate to the Jesus People's interpretation of their parents' attitudes toward them, because of their involvement in the Movement.

How do parents feel about the Jesus Movement?

"The very basis of their hostility comes from fear, 'What has my child gotten in to?' Love is from God, fear is from Satan, and this is manifested in their hostility . . . this fear that they have is for losing their children, perhaps it being a kick, or craze. Although what their children were in before, the drug scene, or the mysticism scene, meditation, hippie life, or even if they were intellectuals like me. They fear that they've lost all control of their senses. But after awhile, it turns out that you reap much reward."

Shelly, San Mateo, California.

"I know several parents that were non-Christians that were very hostile toward their children who had become a part of the Jesus Movement because they believe this to be not educated, but only something the kids were going through."

Mark, Portland, Oregon.

"They think that it's just another fad. I mean, their kid has been through sex and dope and they think that now it's just another thing that is just going to pass away."

Debbie, Campbell, California, Maranatha House.

"They're confused. They don't know what their kids are getting into; they're afraid because they just don't know." *George, Turlock, California, His House.*

"It's a tragic thing that people would get down on their children for becoming Christians, it should be the other way around, and it is in some families, but there is definitely a hostility with ungodly parents and godly children. They don't understand, because they can't understand the things of God."

John, Campbell, California, Agape Force.

"The parents seem to have understood dope and sex a lot better than they understand Jesus, I think that they can compare dope with things in their own lives like booze and sexual encounters they had in their younger lives. They don't understand very much about Jesus. If you have claimed Him as your Lord, they think that you are a fanatic and the spirit of God really has to frighten them because they have to drop their pride and repent for their sins in order to know Jesus as their Lord and many of them don't want to do that."

Cyd, San Francisco, California, Song of Solomon.

"The parents see the change in the child, the difference in attitude. They don't understand it: obviously their first instinct (I don't know why) is to mistrust it, and become hostile."

Bill, San Pablo, California.

"Any way, when I came to Jesus it really blew their minds. The first night with my uncle—he just completely went berserk. He started screaming, 'What did you do that for? You're crazy! I thought you had a brain.' He was just going insane; and I just started to cry, I was so afraid. I just saw Satan in him. The second time it happened, when I first sort of went home, my father went bananas—just started screaming 'What the hell do you need God for?' He was so far gone, my mother was just on the floor crying. And she didn't even remember it happening. For about two minutes he lost his mind. Since that already had happened with my uncle, I perceived it was Satan: his last surge to try and hold me. I just stood up and just took off. And I couldn't cast it out; I was afraid to—I didn't know if it would work. But boy it was heavy."

Eugene, New York, New York.

"I've seen my brothers' and sisters' parents come in to get them and lead them away from serving the Lord at the point of guns; I've seen them break out windows; I've seen them kidnap; I've seen them beat up by their parents; I've seen them drag them away by their hair; I've seen children's parents who were supposedly religious Christians come in with ministers and literally drag their kids away."

Ocem, Hayward, California, Children of God.

"My Mom doesn't understand, she has had a whole bunch of nervous breakdowns. Maybe some day when she is ready, she will be led to a better understanding of God, but I don't think so."

Joel, Hillsboro, California.

"I have had parents tell me that they would rather see their kids in drugs than in Jesus Christ."
Dan, Turlock, California, Leader of the Rapping Post.

"I can't understand why parents wouldn't let their children go to a church. Like, to me it always seemed like it was such a hassle to get your children to go to church, and now, when they really mean business, they say, 'Wow! I don't want my kids going to church. I'd rather have them like they were before.'"

Shauna, Fresno, California, Agape Force.

"I think most parents are concerned with what's happened to the youth today. I think they welcome the change in kids' lives. But I think that they would really welcome it more if they were to see that this change is real and absolute."

Gary, Redwood City, California.

"The hostility breeds from the fact that they don't know what has happened to the kids, they have never confronted it before." *Chuck, Mississippi.*

"My Dad was a year away from becoming the highest order of a Catholic Priest before he married my Mom. He loves God, and he loves the changes that I'm going through." *Joel, Hillsboro, California.*

80

"I think that most parents aren't hostile. It takes awhile for them to realize that their sons and daughters aren't going to rip them off. Most of them are just thankful. I think most of them are grateful for what the Son (Jesus Christ) has done for their children because they're different people."

Sally, Santa Cruz, California, Drug Abuse Preventive Center.

"I don't think parents are opposed to the point of hostility. I've heard more of discomfort and perhaps questions." *Barry, Berkeley, California.*

How far should you go in obeying your parents?

"You should obey your parents all the way I guess, yes, all the way. Just obey them until they get sick of you; they'll get sick of you obeying them after awhile." *Joel, Hillsboro, California.*

"I think parents are trying to do the best for you and you should try as much as possible to always obey them; they're not doing anything that's outlandish—they're not wanting to hurt you. I think if your parents don't make you do anything that's immoral or to go against the law or something, I think you should obey them all the way."

Mark, Redwood City, California.

"One should obey his mother and father to anything that they ask of him. The Bible makes this statement."

Dennis, Turlock, California, Christian House.

"Like in most things you've got to obey your parents, because they are concerned for you. I never used to obey them very much but now I really do. I want my kids to really obey me.

Sally, Santa Cruz, California, Drug Abuse Preventive Center.

"The Bible said, 'even when you think your parents are wrong or tight, you should obey your parents.'"

George, Turlock, California, His House.

"I believe God uses parents, Christian and non-Christian, to develop us as Christians. But, sometimes I use the rationalization—well, my parents aren't Christians so I don't need to obey them.—The old crutch. God is number one, then my parents. But I think God does use the parents. I think in most cases, a lot of maturity has been gotten from parents."

Mark, Portland, Oregon.

"The Bible says that we should honor our father and mother . . . . The son does not rebel against his parents because they are placed there by God; a son should be an obedient son to his parents as he would unto Christ."

Daniel, Campbell, California, Maranatha House.

"As far as I know about obeying parents, I think you should follow them until like they depart from the Gospel or until they depart from the Lord; just follow after God, but not in defiance or rebellion—but in love."

Ann, Campbell, California, Maranatha House.

"Obey your parents until it goes against the moral government that God teaches in the Bible."

Karen, Campbell, California, Agape Force.

"The Bible says to obey all laws of man unless they go against the laws of God. If they tell me to do something the Bible tells me not to I will disobey them because they are disobeying God and the Bible says to love God first and to put Him first. He says and I will have no other gods before me and that is anything even your parents."

Maoch, California, Children of God.

"It depends on the attitudes of the parents; I don't think an 18-year-old child or a 19-year old still at home should have to live totally by his parents' rule. They should start making some of their own decisions, and paying the consequences if they're bad ones."

Bill, San Pablo, California.

"I think children are brought up to obey their parents, but when they get of age able to make their own decisions, and they realize what their parents are asking is totally wrong with their Christian beliefs, they shouldn't have to go along with that."

Kristal, Turlock, California.

"We must remember that our primary responsibility is to God. The parents are the parents of our old man, the new man is fathered by God."

Daniel, Campbell, California, Maranatha House.

"When a couple of kids left their homes to join the force their parents told them not to come back. The Bible says to hate your parents, but not that you hate them, but to choose to serve God rather than people. When you do that, that is what might happen."

Dan, Campbell, California, Leader of Agape Force.

Chapter 7

WHAT SHALL I DO WITH TODAY?

From a casual, outward appearance, the Jesus Movement appears as just another segment of the hippie-type life style of drugs, sex, and a lack of concern for the rest of society. Many of the Jesus People dress radically, wear long hair, live in communes, and share their resources. Few of them have full-time jobs.

A closer examination reveals striking contrasts between Jesus People and familiar hippie types. The Jesus People are influenced in their daily living by the standards and restrictions of the Bible —God's Word, and the word of "elders." The Jesus People are really a separate people.

How should a Christian dress?

"A Christian, like Paul said, has to become all things to all men. I really believe that a Christian has to dress or act or groom himself according to the type of people he witnesses to."

John, El Cajon, California.

"I know myself before I met the Lord, I had a certain type of fashion that I would wear, and wouldn't wear any other fashion because it wasn't my thing. When I became a Christian, I've forsaken the tradition of men, and I've become all things to all men. I'll do anything to save a soul. If I have to put on a suit and tie to win a soul, I'll do that."

Cornelius, Dallas, Texas, Children of God.

"If I was working in a culture in South America, I wouldn't dress the same way I would if I was going to talk to some fraternity men on campus; or if I was going to meet the president of the United States, I would dress an even different way. I think we need to adapt ourselves to the culture."

Anonymous, Berkeley, California, Christian World Liberation Front.

"Look in the Bible. Man, in the Bible it says that John the Baptist dressed in camel's hair and ate locust and wild honey. They wore robes and you could wear anything, you could even go without clothes. Giving away Christ is the important thing."

Ocem, Whyamea, Hawaii, Children of God.

"It doesn't matter what you wear or what you eat or where you sleep or where you live, if your heart's right with the Lord. I just wear what God provides for me."

Rick, Maranatha House.

"Clothes should be practical—keep you warm."

Eugene, New York, New York.

"I like capes and robes and things that flow, and beads and scarves and sashes and so on, gypsy type clothes."   *Byron, Miami, Florida.*

"They should dress according to what they think is beautiful."   *Byron, Miami, Florida.*

"He should dress according to the clothes God gives you."   *Chuck, Vancouver, Canada, Children of God.*

"Christians should just dress anyway they want to. There's no particular style that God approves of, or doesn't approve of. The only rule for dress is modesty."   *C. G., Mill Valley, California, Ivy House.*

"Before I became a Christian I dressed like what you'd say a hippie dresses like. I believe that when you get saved and you turn to the Kingdom of God you should put away all foolishness and dress moderately."
Martin, Campbell, California, House of Uttering.

"I dress pretty straight and I cut my hair just because of a lot of people I work with. It would really hinder their growth in the Lord, and, you know, all things for the glory of God."
George, Jacksonville, Illinois, His House.

"There are no current styles. I believe people should dress the way that God wants them to dress. Sometimes it's with a suit coat and tie on, if they have to meet that type of people; and sometimes it's with nothing on if you have to meet that type of people."
Maoch, Children of God.

"I think people should dress according to whatever they can afford and whatever they feel comfortable in. I don't think that being style-conscious is wrong if one can afford it. If someone is living above their means in order to stay in style, I would say that was wrong."
Bill, San Pablo, California.

How do you get your money?

"We go strictly by faith. We pray in our money. Most of the kids in our group don't have any money. When we do get money, we don't keep over $5.00 a week. We give it to the Force."
Dan, Los Angeles, California, Leader of Agape Force.

"I don't have a regular job—my job is working in this ministry. There are ten of us here. Society is set up so that people who minister like we don't get regular salaries. You have to assume that the ministry of Christ is a valid occupation, and deserves money."
Shauna, Fresno, California, Agape Force.

"Some friends of mine support me and they send me $20.00 a month. That money, I keep it. I don't take it out unless I absolutely need it for something personal or something. We're only allowed to have $5.00 on a week and that's all." *Nancy, Agape Force.*

"I've started selling Christian books so I've invested money in that. I feel it is something of the Lord's work—an investment in the Lord's work. It is something He is leading me and guiding me to do right now, and I give to the church and try to manage my money properly." *Doug, Richmond, California.*

"It's sort of regular, but irregular. It's art work for people; customers want art work, like painting cards, and something like that. They find out through advertising, like a billboard, and other places here."
Robert, Teen Challenge.

"I have sort of a regular job. I am now running a Christian coffee house in this town, which they pay me $100.00 a month plus a room."
Dan, Santa Rosa, California, Rapping Post.

"I have enough money to sustain me day by day; and I've worked in many different ways, and I work for the Lord. He provides everything through faith, and I'm truly living on faith."

Kyle, Berkeley, California, Resurrection City.

"I teach piano about twice a week if that is counted as a regular job."   *Kristal, San Mateo, California.*

"The Bible says don't be lazy; if you don't work, don't eat. I believe it in my heart. I work and I pray that my life is an example. If a man is faithful to the Lord, he will work, even for no money. God will supply the food for him, and he will be able to give to others so that God will supply somebody else's needs, as well as our own."

Nick, Turlock, California, His House.

"I work, and I work from 8 to 12, and I support myself and a couple other people—a couple other Christians. If the Lord doesn't want them to work because I can support them, praise the Lord. If somebody were to support me, praise the Lord. The Lord takes care of me."

George, Jacksonville, Illinois, His House.

"Yes, I have a regular job. I work here in the Vega Hut which is a Christian restaurant and it's a ministry to the people in this area. I don't receive any wages."

Steven, Mountain View, California.

How do you spend your money?

"I give my tithe and offering, and I help out here at the Church. I don't spend too much on myself: I pay a little bit of rent at home, and I put the rest in the bank."   *Shelley, San Mateo, California.*

"Donate it to the ministry of the Lord and what I don't I usually spend on my flesh."   *Anonymous.*

"The money that we get we pay for food, rent, insurance on our cars, to move around and minister in places—just our basic needs. We go out to restaurants sometimes: take a vacation about twice a year."

C. G., Mill Valley, California, Ivy House.

"It goes to the Lord to be channeled through the ministry of the Christian House—whatever the Lord lays on my heart."

Dennis, Whittier, California, Christian House.

"The Bible says, 'Silver and gold have I none; but such as I have give I thee.' The fact is that when it says that we must forsake all, it means to forsake all and have all things common. And I don't have any money." *Ocem, Whyamea, Hawaii, Children of God.*

"I give it to the House here so we can eat, and if a brother needs some money, I'll give him the money. It's all the Lord's money—everything is the Lord's."

Rick, Maranatha House.

How much money do you have totally?

"About $300 in my savings."

Teresa, San Mateo, California.

"Not enough."   *Bill, San Pablo, California.*

"About 25 cents right now. Give or take a penny."

Richard, Turlock, California.

"$400 in my savings." *Sandra, Sunnyvale, California.*

"Approximately $12." *Anonymous.*

"Well, I have 50 cents."

C. G., Mill Valley, California, Ivy House.

"Just under $40."
Christopher, Berkeley, California, House of Ebeneser.

"12 cents." *Karen, Reedley, California, Agape.*

"A penny and one peso." *Dan, Merced, California.*

"About $2.00." *Mary, Turlock, California.*

"$25.00." *Eugene, New York, New York.*

"6 cents." *Chuck, San Jose, California, House of Maranatha.*

"A dollar." *Ronald, San Francisco, California.*

"I make about $250.00 a month." *Nick, Turlock, California.*

"I'm living on welfare." *Bill, San Pablo, California.*

"Right now I have about 60 cents." *Gary, San Francisco, California.*

"Right now I have about $50, I just got paid."
Dan, Santa Rosa, California.

"I haven't got a cent." *Anonymous.*
"I have about $300 and I just quit my work, I'm going to get married, and I'm not worried."
Steve, Thorton, California, The Christian House.

How do you feel about living in communes?

"I don't know what the Socialists are but the Bible talks about communal living as it's called; living together, sharing all of the things that you have. This is the way the Bible preaches it. This is the way they told you to live from Adam right on down to the book of Revelation."
Maoch, Southern California, Children of God.

"I've lived in communal situations for the last two years now. I really like communal living. I've found

90

that most Christian houses are kind of like boot camp in the Navy. I was made from a super civilian to a super military man within three months. I think that a lot of these new Christians need this heavy training of discipline of the flesh; in fact just understanding just what God wants and requires of you in these first three months in heavy communal living is really good for them. Several things happen when you are living together. You are forced to maintain a much more spiritual relationship with God."

Dan, Santa Rosa, California, Rapping Post.

"We are concerned with people's physical needs. Look at the Jesus People communes that feed and house anybody in need."   *Gary.*

"I know that we have been accused of being communists. I believe it is somewhat because everybody is on a sharing basis and it is a communal-type trip. But I believe we depend very much on the free enterprise system."   *Joe, San Leandro, California,*
Drug Prevention Abuse Center.

"I think it's really far out. You really learn a lot about giving and day-to-day living."

Micky, New Jersey.

"It can really show you how to love people and it can be very economical. When it gets hectic it can really detract from the Christian life."

Steve, Mountain View, California.

"I've learned more just with my own personal relationship walking with God than I could ever learn in a commune, with the 6 months in the mountains. He has put us here for a reason, to share Christ with other people, not just to bottle Him up in some commune, stuck away somewhere."

Bob, El Cajon, California.

"I don't really believe in the idea as a Christian. I think God made a cooperative situation which is very different, but which allows the person's privacy."

Howard.

"First of all, I don't live in a commune. I believe that God ordained each family, the husband and wife, as a unit—and each family unit must be maintained. And I also believe that communal living is good as a temporary thing for single people, but it's not a good practice for married people with families."

Anonymous.

What about children in communal living? Is it detrimental for them?

"It's not detrimental at all; it's God's commandment that we live together.

Cornelius, Dallas, Texas, Children of God.

"It depends what kind of commune it is. Like if you're in a commune with a lot of different Christian people, I don't think it could hurt them at all."

Anonymous.

"I think it would be a good idea because your children would have playmates that live right there, and they would get used to having adults around."

Teresa, San Mateo, California, The Way Inn.

"It can be very bad for little kids not having a real family life." Kristal, San Mateo, California.

How do you feel about higher education?

"Becoming a Christian doesn't mean you have to throw away your brain." Bob, El Cajon, California.

"There are certain skills which have to be learned and sometimes the best means of learning them on earth is in a higher education."   *Micky, New Jersey.*

"A higher education for a Christian is good if that is what God wants you to have. I think that educated Christians is what we need more of in the world."
John, El Cajon, California.

"I believe that if God leads you to go to school, you should go to school but you should discern out what is true knowledge and what is man's wisdom."
Dan, Merced, California, A Christian House.

"I don't think Christians should have to be dummies. We encourage our people to finish high school."
Sally, Washington, Drug Abuse Prevention Center.

"I myself am very socially conscious. I feel that there are many ills in this world that need to be remedied. Education is certainly one way of at least attempting to do so. If every Christian quit high school, then there would be no one in a position to talk to any one above that level except by chance on the street-type thing."   *Bill, San Pablo, California.*

"I quit college after three and a half years and I'm glad, because the only thing that's going to stand is God's Word."
Steve, Thornton, California, Turlock Christian House.

"You just get all wrapped up in man's vain philosophies."   *Keith, Sunnyvale, California.*

"I'd rather get my spiritual scholarship in life."
Steve, Thornton, California, Turlock Christian House.

"Well, I think that there's a value in school, but I've learned more in my walk with Jesus in the last year, being out of school."   *Kyle, Berkeley, California.*

"Well, it says that if anyone lack wisdom, let him ask of God that giveth to all man liberally and it shall be given him. I went to college and it didn't get me nowhere."

Shiela, Santa Barbara, California, Children of God.

"I've had four years of college, and I've been out of college about two years; and I have learned more from God about people, about living in the world, about even just the process of learning."

Shelley, San Mateo, California.

"Our present school system and education system is not set up to teach the wisdom of God. The Bible also says that the wisdom of man is foolishness in the eyes of God. If you want higher wisdom, seek God, and learn the eternal things of God, and you'll have eternal treasures in Heaven."

C. G., Mill Valley, California, Ivy House.

"When I think of higher education, there is only one high education in my books, that is the Holy Word of God."   *Dan, Santa Rosa, California, Rapping Post.*

"I'm not in school. I decided not to go to college. It was a big decision to make. I already had made plans to go to college before I was a Christian but when I became a Christian I went directly into the ministry, I thought about going to Bible college, but the Lord decided to put me in a different area. In fact, I think I learned more here than I would in college because I was constantly studying."

Dan, Los Angeles, California, Leader of Agape Force.

"I go to school every day in the Lord, because I study my Bible and that's my school."

George, Jacksonville, Illinois, His House.

"All you need to know is the Bible. Why learn about anything else but the Bible?"

Maoch, Hayward, California, Children of God.

What about Christian schools, Bible colleges, and seminaries —do you approve?

"I'm going to seminary because I believe it can help me to know the Word and I need a spiritual environment. To say that seminary is necessarily spiritual—I think there are very few that are really Christ-centered now days. I think Bible school and Christian college are only good to the point by which kids can get to know the Lord and can be well-founded."

Mark, Portland, Oregon.

"It is important for Christians to be grounded and taught in the Word of God, and not just any doctrine. I think Bible colleges are really good."

Debbie, Campbell, California, Maranatha House.

"I think that it's great if it's led by the Holy Spirit, and it's not misused and intellectualized."

Kyle, Berkeley, California, Resurrection City.

"I think accurate knowledge of the Word of God is the need for this day and time. As far as seminary and organization goes, I haven't seen a Bible college yet that really fulfills a need."

Steven, Alameda, California, The Way.

"I've never been. My frank opinion is that if you had much of Jesus when you began you might end up without it . . . the spirit isn't there."   *Richard.*

"You can take your theology and your doctrine, and you can throw it out the window. I don't want to be bothered with it, if it's not in the Bible as it's printed. I don't need no man's interpretation of the Bible for me."   *Newton, San Francisco, California.*

"Seek direct revelation from Jesus, that's the only knowledge that lasts. Here's us, you know, in the drug scene, heroin addicts and all this and momentum that we carry is even greater than them."

Danny, Redwood City, California, House of Manna.

"That's one of the Devil's tools to get you involved with the system. Because most people who went to seminary don't even believe the Bible. And most people who get a higher education don't even believe the Bible. So it's all Satan's instrument."

Cornelius, Hayward, California, Children of God.

"Well, I went to a Bible college and I never looked at a Bible while I was there. All I had were books that man wrote about the Bible. I don't need to listen to man to see what he says."

Shiela, Hayward, California, Children of God.

"I think most seminaries are perpetuating a form of religion that doesn't have any power in it. And I think that if most of the seminaries were closed down, it would do the cause of Christianity a lot of good."

Anonymous, Berkeley, CWLF.

"Well, I hate to use these words but I sometimes say Bible Cemeteries, because in most cases they're so liberal, and so much of secular understanding and secular teachings in there because the Devil has gotten in." *Dan, Turlock, California, Rapping Post.*

"I know if Jesus calls me to be a pastor, I'm going to be a pastor. You don't need no Bible college or nothing and I'm free to do anything. We should be led completely of the Spirit."

Danny, Redwood City, California, House of Manna.

"I think seminaries are becoming like the institutionalized church. It is so bent to the world's programming that it is very difficult to find a seminary where the Christian can learn more about the Bible, learn more about evangelism, and learn more about preaching." *Doug, Richmond, California.*

Do you like Rock Music?

"Music does not heighten the awareness of spiritual things but rather the awareness of fleshly things."
C. G., Mill Valley, California, Ivy House.

"Yeah, my flesh really goes for it."
Ann, Los Gatos, California. Maranatha House.

"I don't like what it does. It makes me be like I used to be: plastic, cool, far out, let's get out the joints."
Steve, Berkeley, California.

"It doesn't really attract me at all. Two years ago I was really involved in rock and roll music or acid rock but now I find that I can't even stand listening to it."
Dan, Santa Rosa, California, Rapping Post.

"I used to be a rock musician, and I know where that game is coming from. It's a pulsating beat, and it's a very sexually heavy trip; and I think that the farther away you get from the real hard beat the better it is."
Kyle, Berkeley, California, Resurrection City.

"I think it can be good. I have heard some things about rock music. It can do things to your mind, like certain beats can get you into different moods, and I think I heard a quote from some man that they're using this to get the kids in their revolution, and that's why you have to be really careful, I think."
Janice, Fresno, California. Agape Force.

"I like the freshness and spontaneity of it, how it can sort of eminate from our spirits and from our souls. It doesn't heighten my spirituality."
Micky, New Jersey.

"No, I don't like it because there's not anything about Christ in it. There's nothing in there that would even make me stop and think about Him and who He is and what He's doing. It makes you think about the hate in the world, the violence in the world, the love between men and men and women and women, and the songs are of it."

Nancy, San Jose, California, Agape House.

"My flesh, which I don't like, and rock music is really bumming me out. I used to be hung up on it, dig it, and jam to it, and now I just really would rather have more music that's of the Spirit."

Steve, Thornton, California.

What do you think about Christian Rock Music?

"Christian rock music is like worldly music; I like it because I can dig the beat, but I don't like it when it gets too loud and you can't understand the words because a lot of it can distort people. If the music gets over-powering and you can't get what they're saying about the Gospel. My mind just cuts off right there. My mind just says wow, I don't think God is pleased with a person jamming it and here you are just digging on the beat." *Sandra, Sunnyvale, California.*

"I like Christian rock to an extent. This ministry has a bunch of musicians that are into recording. I find that some are a little off in their doctrine. It is just what we were raised on. It does not heighten your awareness of spiritual things." *Steven, Hillsborough.*

"I like any music God can use to win souls, as long as it's for the glory of God and not for the glory of the person who is playing it. I know when I was in church nobody ever got alive with the songs there. But I know we even have slow songs and they are really beautiful."

Shiela, Santa Barbara, California, Children of God.

"We use rock style to reach kids that we have a message for. The message is more important. We use rock style because it's more alive and it reaches more kids than the conventional hymns that we have in church."   *Cornelius, Dallas, Texas.*

"It depends on what kind of Christian rock it is, like acid rock is totally a hindrance. I believe that God's wrath is upon that kind of music. It's one of Satan's heaviest works with the young people in these last days. A lot of Christians today, they get saved and they'll take John Lennon's music and put Jesus Christ in front of it. I disagree with it . . ."
Martin, Campbell, California.

"It seems that rock music came about the same time as the drug culture. It's sort of going hand in hand— rock music goes hand in hand with the taking of drugs and putting it in the name of the Lord is sometimes not advisable."   *Doug, Richmond, California.*

"I have heard some very beautiful heavy songs written by Christian groups. There are some written by people in our own group. Sometimes it's just half way between. It's all very beautiful music if it glorifies God. The Bible says whether therefore ye eat or drink or whatsoever ye do, do all to the glory of God."
Maoch, Southern California, Children of God.

"I feel that Christian rock music, can be and is used in many churches, as a way of captivating young people. If it's the same drone that's used in the drug culture, we don't allow it in this home, because of its affect on the mind, drawing it back to times when they were in that droning atmosphere, shooting up."
Amy, San Martin, California, Girls Teen Challenge.

What do you enjoy doing most?

"I think a Christian to relax must be in peace with the Lord. I believe that a Christian who has fellowship with the Lord is going to be relaxed, is going to be much calmer than he was when he wasn't a Christian. I think that prayer helps us to calm ourselves. I think that fellowship with other Christians helps us."

Doug, Richmond, California.

"Jesus says, 'Come unto me, all that labor and are heavy laden and I shall give thee rest unto thy soul.' A real Christian has rest when he's in the will of God; serving God is the only real rest."

Cornelius, Children of God.

"Today I started drawing, but I think the best relaxation of all is realizing what Ephesians says, I think in the 3rd chapter, that we are seated together with Christ Jesus and that we are more than conquerors. I think the heaviest form of relaxation is just realizing that we are seated with Christ and that we don't have to do anything but that He will do everything."   *Tim, Menlo Park, California.*

"I think we should rest in the Lord, and I think we can rest in the Lord every minute of every day, and I think that's relaxation."

Steve, Mountain View, California.

"There is all kinds of thing. We do a lot of things; we live very normal lives. We'll go out together and play volleyball, or basketball, or go to the movies— light movies, nothing we wouldn't be able to enjoy."
Sally, Santa Cruz, California, Drug Abuse Prevention Center.

"Well, there's lots of things you can do, like personally I ride my horse and do things like that, you know. It's normal."   *Anonymous.*

"If you've been under emotional pressure, or something, go to the mountains—take a vacation. Most pressure comes from being around people. The best thing to do is to leave people. If you like different sports or something, do that."

> C. G., Mill Valley, California, Ivy House.

"Yoga, swimming, sauna baths, fornication, whatever . . ." Byron, Miami, Florida.

"Preaching the Gospel, telling others about Christ, going out and seeing souls won for Christ, seeing a life change, seeing somebody that didn't have the truth accept the truth. Someone who was dead spiritually become born as a new-born child because life is beautiful."

> Maoch, Southern California, Children of God.

"If I'm not living Jesus Christ, talking Jesus Christ, sharing Jesus Christ, working with my brothers in this ministry, then I am unhappy. This is my life, and my life is Jesus Christ."

> Nick, Turlock, California, Leader of His House.

"Praising God and just fellowshipping with brothers and sisters. There's just so much joy when fellowshipping with brothers and sisters."

> Rich, Campbell, California, Maranatha House.

"Honestly, to express it in a human term I couldn't. The thing which I enjoy the most is serving God, worshiping the Lord."

> Daniel, Maranatha House.

"Driving and flying."

> Dennis, Whittier, California, Christian House.

"Drawing."

> Joe, Santa Cruz, California, Drug Abuse Prevention Center.

"Just talking about God and reading my Bible."

> Richard, Turlock, California.

"Being with my husband."

Sally, Drug Abuse Prevention Center.

"That's a difficult question. Depends on where my head's at. I like acid more than anything else in the world." *Byron, Miami, Florida.*

"I think that the time that I feel really the best all the way around is when I've had like a half hour in communication with God getting things straightened out with Him and me and just talking to Him and stuff because He understands the best."

Sandra, Sunnyvale, California.

Chapter 8

AM I ALLOWED TO DO THAT?

The youth culture of today has been centered around drugs. The Jesus Revolution has taken an active leadership role toward finding a solution for this plague. In this chapter you will find comments about how the Movement encounters and handles not only the drug scene, but also two other debasements of our society: rising homosexuality and alcoholic beverages.

Why do people get into drugs?

"It stems from a lack of love, a lack of truth, a lack of understanding the Scriptures, and not accepting Jesus Christ as their Savior." *Kristal.*

"Well, there are many reasons why they get involved in the drug scene. We are living in a kicks-oriented society, and everybody wants some kicks. And even though I think a lot of young people know that drugs aren't good for them, they believe that Satanic lie, 'It won't happen to me. It'll happen to everyone else, but I'll never get hooked. I'll smoke a joint once in awhile, take a few reds once in awhile, but I'm not going to push a needle in my arm that's crazy.' "

Richard, Los Angeles, California. Teen Challenge.

Can drug addiction be cured?

"When Christ came in my heart He lifted a tremendous burden off of my heart. I looked at this same burden to be lifted off in every form of drug that I took. When Christ says, 'Come unto me all ye that are heavy laden and I will give you rest,' that is a tremendous feeling."   *Dan, Santa Rosa, California.*

"People in this day and age are realizing that they need something beyond themselves—something spiritual. A lot of them have this revealed to them by having taken drugs. They realize there is a spiritual realm. They realize that there is a power in the spiritual realm, and receive Christ, as fulfilling this need."   *Shelly, San Mateo, California.*

"The boys use the term, 'It's gonna take a little while for the Lord to put my head together.' Our cure rate here ranges from—let me put it this way: 50% of the boys who come into our program here within the first two weeks, they leave. They do not stay. We can't help them, of course, out on the streets. But the 50% that do stay in the program, the cure rate is from 74% to 93%—that's pretty high."

Richard, Los Angeles, California, Teen Challenge.

What about Christians and drugs; should Christians use them?

"No, I don't think so. Drugs are a tool used by Satan, and is a great handicap to the Christian life."
Nick, Turlock, California.

"I've never seen a Christian in my experience, who drugs have helped. Some claim that they have found Christ in LSD, but I am very skeptical of this."
Mark, Portland, Oregon.

"I feel that it is just the opposite of a help to your Christian walk. In fact, it destroys your spiritual relationship with Christ."
Dan, Santa Rosa, California.

104

"Yes, I do know Christians involved in drugs, and I think that they have misinterpreted what the Gospel meant to be 'high,' and I think that being high on drugs is no closer to God than just waking up in the morning."   *Kyle, Berkeley, California.*

"No. Drugs, along with sexual immorality, will hamper the relationship with Christ; will sever it."
                    Doug, Richmond, California.

"Paul says, 'All things are lawful but not all things are expedient.' I don't think drugs helped anyone see God more clearly."   *Dan, Merced, California.*

What do you think about homosexuality? Do you think there is an increase in it?

"Homosexuality is just a prophecy that is being fulfilled. Homosexuality is more now than it ever has been. In all of the years that it has been here it has just multiplied; now more in the last days than it ever has. They're just hungry people just trying to fill that emptiness inside with sex."
                    Martin, Campbell, California.

"The Bible teaches that a homosexual will not inherit the kingdom of God."
                    James, New York, New York.

"Relationships are supposed to be not only physically healthy between two people, but also psychologically, socially, spiritually. In any of these areas if this planned relationship deviates from God's law then it becomes perversion." *Dan, Redwood City, California.*

"It states definitely in the Bible that homosexuality is abnormal. It's not of God; it has no place at all in a Christian Church."   *Phil, San Mateo, California.*

"He destroyed a whole city because of it."

Sheila, Santa Barbara, California.

"Well, that was the sin of Sodom and Gomorrah, and God destroyed them for it. America has the same sin as it is talked about in Romans chapter one; it says that we 'change the truth of God into a lie and worship and serve the creature rather than the creator who is blessed forever, Amen. For this cause shall God deliver them unto vile affection. Their women exchanged the natural use of their bodies for that which is against nature and likewise their men, leaving the natural use of the women, turning their lust one toward another. Men working that which is unseemly and receiving in themselves that recompence for their error which was made.' So, it is against God's Word. Man, if it's completely against God's Word—God killed people for it and God destroyed nations for it—America is no different, and He is going to destroy it, too."

Ocem, Whyamea, Hawaii.

"I think that if the established church starts or is justifying the practice of homosexuality, it is a sign that the church is reprobate and is given over to Satanic forces."

Christopher, Berkeley, California.

"Christ says that they must be born again, and He will be the answer for their needs."

Shelly, San Mateo, California.

"According to Romans 1, homosexuality is just another manifestation of man's need of God. When you can't make love with God, you start making love with other things, such as education, and cars, and anything. So that's just another manifestation of lack of love for God. I know myself. I've been involved in homosexuality before I met the Lord. So when I found the love of the Lord, I didn't need it."

Cornelius, Dallas, Texas.

"I have a burden for the homosexual kids because unless they ask Jesus Christ into their lives and ask Jesus to change these unnatural desires, they are going to burn in Hell. I used to be a male prostitute before I had my face rearranged with a crowbar. So, that's why I have such a burden for these kids, because I was in it. Christ delivered me from it."

Newton, San Francisco, California.

"I feel negatively about it, but I don't just put a stamp on it and throw it to the pit. I mean, it's a disease, . . . and I think it can be cured by Christ."

Eugene, New York, New York.

"I feel that if I was a homosexual and I knew that it was wrong, I would just wait on the Lord."

Joel, Hillsboro, California.

"People who are bound by homosexuality, I think they are demon-possessed, just like a person on drugs. Once a person's delivered from that, I think he'll straighten up, but he has to want to be delivered. That's the thing." *Gary, Redwood City, California.*

"Homosexuality is a sin in the eyes of God and has to be looked at as sin, and also as a disease—a trap that someone could be ensnared in kind of unwillingly. A person has to be willing to come out of it, like any other sin." *C.G., Mill Valley, California.*

Should a Christian abstain from alcoholic beverages?

"I feel that alcohol is a great device that the Devil uses to keep us away from God. Because I was an alcoholic and I can see how that if I had even a drink or two, it will break down that spiritual realm that I have over my head, and I can just feel demons come in and deceive me." *Gary, San Francisco, California.*

107

"I don't think they should abstain. I don't think Christians should abstain unless the Lord convicts them."   *Micky, New Jersey.*

"I drank almost continually for ten years and almost was considered an alcoholic, but since I came to the Lord, it's been very seldom times that I have ever sipped a beer."   *Dan, Santa Rosa, California.*

"We should rather be drunk or rather filled with the spirit by singing and giving thanks and this kind of thing. Getting drunk, you lose your perception and you're not as able to make clear judgment."
                                          Bob, El Cajon, California.

"I think in today's society, alcoholic beverages usually do cause people to stumble. I don't feel alcoholic beverages, in themselves, are a sin. At least, I don't think they are; but I think unfortunately, most people don't know how to use them. I've very seldomly seen a Christian have a testimony who is drinking—with a beer in one hand and witnessing about Jesus Christ with the other."   *Mark, Portland, Oregon.*

"It says that if you are sick, then alcohol is good for you. If I had a stomachache or something I can see the justifications for it. There are other things you can use now, and I think, basically, the Christian should not use it; because the non-Christian looks at it and he feels that the Christian shouldn't drink. The majority of them do I don't think a Christian should drink."
                                          Dan, Los Angeles, California.

"I drink, but not in excess like some people do. I like wine and I love the taste of it. I think people should try to give it up as much as possible, but not enough to quit; just enough to enjoy themselves and be merry in the Lord."

                                          Rock, Richmond, California.

"The Bible says what use alcohol has in the Christian's life. Paul told Timothy to use a little wine for our stomach's sake and it says, 'Be not drunk with wine wherein is excess, but be filled with the Spirit.' A little bit of wine never hurt anybody."

Rekum, Santa Barbara, California.

"You can drink wine, the Bible says; but as long as you don't get drunk; as long as you don't get high, because when you get high, it's a sin. You should drink wine with your Thanksgiving dinner or things like that."

Chuck.

Chapter 9

DO THE JESUS PEOPLE SPOOK OUT?

If there is a God, and His Word is true, then there must be His counter-part—Satan.

Orthodox Christianity labels the world of the occult—witches, astrology, and demons in the same league with works of the Devil. This chapter will help you find out what the Jesus Ones say about the Black Arts and their Daddy.

Who is Satan?

"In the New Testament, he's a bad dude."

Bob, El Cajon, California.

"Satan is actually a fallen angel. He is a power on earth; he is a spirit, too. He is the spirit of evil."

Joe, Santa Cruz, California,
Drug Abuse Preventive Center.

"Satan is the God of this world."

Daniel, San Jose, California, Maranatha House.

"He was created by God as an angel, and very high in God's dominion. But when this very height of his power caused him to have pride, he said, 'I will exalt myself above the throne of God.' And God said, in words, 'Now look: I just can't have this exaltation above Me, because it's not true—it's a lie. And this lie that you've told yourself is sin, and it's not true, and it's the opposite of light. It's darkness, and I cannot have darkness in My Kingdom. You'll just have to leave.' There's something about the holiness of God that does not allow sin in His presence."

Shelly, San Mateo, California.

"He's the person that used to rule my life."
Steve, Thorton, California, The Christian House of Turlock.

"Most of the time I can't tell if it is Satan or me who wants to do things."

Mary, Turlock, California, His House.

"Satan is Lucifer, which is another name for him. He was the head of the choir in Heaven, but he got his ego in the way and he and the whole choir got kicked out of Heaven. He is the serpent, snake, beast."

Newton, San Francisco, California.

"He's the enemy of God. He's the destroyer of Christians. He's the prince of darkness. He's evil."

Nancy, Reedley, California, Agape.

"All those who say there is no such thing as God, or spirits, or anything, are practicing Satan, just by their openness. Satan is blindness and darkness."

Eugene, New York, New York.

"Satan is our enemy; he is a fallen angel. To me, he just tries to make my Christian life very hard."

Debbie, Massachusetts, Maranatha House.

"He is a defeated foe, and he knows his time is short." *Kirk, Douglas, Arizona.*

How does Satan manifest himself?

"There are Satanic forces which are always at work, and they are very strong forces, that if you don't call upon Christ, these forces will probably be the forces

111

that dominate your life, such as the kind of life that I was involved in while taking drugs, being anti-establishment and anti-society." *Susan, Minnesota.*

"He manifests himself as he is. Like, he's a spirit; and sometimes he comes as a good guy, as an angel of light. To the Christian he comes as one who's an accuser—like, in my case, he tries to bring trouble up from my past and accuse me of it—make me feel guilty." *Mildred, Los Angeles.*

"Very subtly. Most of the methods that Satan uses to confuse and tempt can be very beautiful and very alert. He's not at all the enemy of God, but the uplifter and edifier of man."
Bill, San Pablo, California.

"Satan manifests himself in selfishness. I think behind every basic sin in the world today you'll find a foundation and the foundation is selfishness."
Gary, Redwood City, California.

"He looks good, appears good, and just creeps in and starts controlling you. You're not aware of it."
Steve, Thorton, California, The Christian House.

"I would say he manifests himself in every thing you can think of: hatred, frustration, deceit, lust, dishonesty, envy, avarice; all the sins which really are thoughts."
Kyle, Berkeley, California, Resurrection City.

"I imagine that Satan is a very strategic individual —he probably works on people in areas of influence. He doesn't always come as a roaring lion or a bogeyman, but he comes many times as an angel of light. He comes in the form of religion, but he denies always the power of Jesus."
Anonymous, Berkeley, California, Christian World Liberation Front.

"He feeds off sin, and sin is a spiritually inherited gene which everybody has whether they know it or not."   *Tim, Menlo Park, California.*

"Through worldly desires such as alcohol, sex, perversion of any one thing, anything like that; and he grows in you."   *Phil, San Mateo, California.*

"Anyone who contradicts the Bible is being used by Satan."
                    James, New York, New York, Teen Challenge.

"He manifests himself in countless numbers of ways—war, hatred, sickness; all the downers that life has to offer."
                    Stephen, San Francisco, California, The Way.

What are demons?

"I think he (Satan) also has helpers—demons."
                    Janice, Fresno, California.

"You don't see demons. They manifest themselves through people, and they bring people into spiritual bondage and they affect them."
                    Daniel, San Jose, California, Maranatha House.

"I've seen a lot of people, including myself, when they've had Satan using them, and there was a certain amount of evil forces working in them. If you want to call it a demon, I guess you could."
                    Terry, Redwood City, California.

"It's like a personality inside them that's not really them."   *Shelley, San Mateo, California.*

"Upon talking to Pastor when I was present when he cast out three demons, he said that it was a very 'icy' feeling. He had his hand on the person, and he said it felt like ice water going through him. There was no love. He felt no real love—just a hate."
                    Amy, Martin, California, Teen Challenge.

"To me there is no difference between having a demon and worrying about whether you have one or not."
Joel, Hillsboro, California.

Are demons real? Have you seen one? How could you tell?

"Yes, I have. There was a guy that was in here a couple of months ago who was Pan reincarnated, so he said. He brought in a girl one day that was wandering up and down the street; she was really, really kinda like she was tripped out. Not like she was on dope, necessarily, but like, he said she had a demon, you know, and as soon as he started talking about it she fell off the chair and started convulsing on the floor. That was heavy, man, I tell ya."
Steve, Mountain View, California.

"Yeah, I was a participant in a very heavy service one night, where we had this man come in; and then it came down to the salvation message and this guy was very open to receiving the Lord. Yet, there was something that was really tormenting him. His hands became very rigid and he started cringing and shaking, and one of the brothers went over and laid his hands on his head and immediately this force—this demon that was inside of the guy—actually picked him up right out of his chair and threw him, face first, down on the ground and started screaming this tormented scream. It sounded like they were coming out of Hell. About three or four of us rushed down to the guy. The Devil was trying to choke the guy and kill him, and we just got him together, and in the name of Jesus, and commanded it to come out of the man. Within about a minute, it just popped right out and was gone. The guy was filled with the Holy Spirit and was just so in love with Jesus."
Tim, Menlo Park, California.

114

"I have a gift of discernment. So God tells me who has demons, and sometimes He tells me what the names of the demons are."
Christopher, Berkeley, California, House of Ebenezer.

"Yeah, once a sister named Andrea was living here—and we were all in the church, and she knew she was possessed. She goes, 'I know I'm possessed.' In the morning she was purple—her whole body was purple; and her eyes, they looked so haunted you could almost see the demons within her. And later on that night we all gathered around and prayed for her, and we just cast out Satan. We asked the Devil what his name was and all of a sudden she said, 'I hate'; and we said, 'Alright, in the name of Jesus Christ of Nazareth, Hate Demon, we cast you out. Go back to the gates of Hell.' And all of a sudden a scream came out of her, and it was just like a murderous scream, really frantic. And she looked a little better but she goes, 'I still have one within me. I can feel it.' And so we go, 'Alright, what's your name, Demon?' And she said, 'I'm afraid.' We said, 'Fear Demon, we bind you and we cast you out of her.' And it came out of her, and she yelled again with the same shrieking yell, and it was just really scary. But after that she was just like her old self—full of love, full of Jesus."
Gary, San Francisco, California.

"Yes, I think so. A lady at church one time, and I was praying for her. (HOW COULD YOU TELL SHE WAS POSSESSED?) She told us herself that she was. She was choking or gagging. Then other people came. She was foaming at the mouth. That necessarily doesn't mean that those particular things have to happen. I think you can also have a glare in your eyes or something." *Janice, Fresno, California.*

"I haven't had the opportunity to cast out demons. I've been in deliverance sessions, and I've seen demons cast out, but the Bible tells us that we can cast demons out in the name of Jesus."

Anonymous, San Pablo, California.

"Well, they weren't the kind you'd normally think of as someone having a demon, to be really crazy or possessed. We've had people come here who've been really possessed by a demon. I'd have to say that I've seen people possessed by demons. (HOW COULD YOU TELL?) Just by looking in their eyes, or the way they acted. The person had to be watched every minute— you didn't know what they were going to do next, because they might hurt someone, or hurt themselves."

Susan, Minneapolis, Minnesota.

Are demons unreal?

"I have commanded darkness to be cast out many times. As far as demons go, you have to be kind of careful. A lot of people talk about demons and all this other stuff, and a lot of times they don't know what they are talking about."

Neal, Detroit, Michigan.

"I've seen people in the world that I've known to have demons. I've seen them cast out before, supposedly. But I don't know if it was real or if it was emotional. But I know that there are demons."

Mike, Salt Lake City, Utah.

"I've seen people who have supposedly cast out demons. But I've had some doubts about them, whether they really know what they're doing."

Steve, Berkeley, California.

What is a witch? What do witches do?

"Oh, everybody's a witch or a wizard to some degree. I know a few powerful ones, just about two or three. Everyone has potential power."

Byron, San Francisco, California.

"Before I came to the Center I wasn't involved in witchcraft. My friends were just beginning to get interested in sort of adverse things—things I really couldn't go along with because they seemed to be getting into such a weird thing. Like they were getting so heavily into drugs that when drugs didn't satisfy them, that's when they were exposed to witchcraft."

Sally, Santa Cruz, California,
Drug Abuse Preventive Center.

"I have never known any witches personally except on Halloween. I hope I never meet any; if I do, I'll tell them about Jesus." *Anonymous, San Jose, California.*

"I don't know any witches, to tell you the truth. I don't know exactly what a witch is."

Mark, Portland, Oregon.

"I've met one who was a witch and has become a Christian. I met a warlock who has become a Christian. There's another girl whose mother holds seances, so I suppose she might consider herself a witch. They claim to have power. Personally, I've never seen any of that power manifested towards me. Most of it is talk." *Shelley, San Mateo, California.*

"When you get into the concept of witchcraft and the whiter cult and blacker cult, people are messing around with something that I don't think they know what they're getting into. It's scary."

Terry, Redwood City, California.

"I met a girl in school that professes to be a witch. She believes in Satan and has told me that she has sold her soul to the Devil. She does commune with Satan."
Doug, Spring Valley, California.

"My brother's wife and my brother; he's pretty messed up. He's a warlock to witchcraft, too. (HOW

DO YOU KNOW THEY'RE WITCHES?) Well, they're just pulled away by Satanic powers."

Mark, Redwood City, California.

How can you tell they are witches?

"If they're into witchcraft really heavy, sometimes it's hard to tell if they are, unless they tell you that they are. See, because Satan has a duplicate of anything that God has, except for the fullness; you can't receive full peace and joy from Satan." *Anonymous.*

"I don't know them personally, but I have met a few. People talk about witches, like at Halloween, with the witches and pumpkins and the witchcraft, and they just think that it is a phony-like thing. They read about the Salem witch trials and the witches, and they don't understand that there is a power, and it's real. Like up in the Santa Cruz mountains I've seen like, some of their sacrifices, like cats and things that they decapitate the heads and use them in their rites and rituals. It's real."

Rick, Campbell, California, Maranatha House.

"Before I was saved, I was a warlock. I was heavily into Black Magic for the money. There is good money in it if you can find people who are sucker enough to your garbage which you peddle. That's all I was doing it for was the money. Because I didn't believe in contrary Spirits, I didn't believe in Satan, and I didn't believe in Jesus. I was a flat agnostic."

Newton, San Francisco, California.

What part does Satan play in the Occult?

"We see Satan's powers manifested in witchcraft. You will be amazed and astounded at the ways and the real powers that these witchcrafters have. I've talked to some kids who have had some very real and frightening experiences with seances and things of this nature. Some people don't believe that God's power is working or moving anymore and that there are experiences in black magic and with the occult. If the dark powers are moving, then surely God's power is moving too."   *John, Whittier, California.*

"I've lived in a lot of places where I'd guess you'd say there was 'Black Magic' being practiced. There's a girl here that used to be a witch, and she was really able to control people's minds."
                    Susan, Minneapolis, Minnesota.

"The way to get possessed by spirits would be by yielding to them; giving place to the Devil by going into such things as astrology, witchcraft; by going into tarot cards, horoscopes, ESP, because they are all means by which the Devil enters into man, and controls him."   *Anonymous.*

"Astrology is being used as one of Satan's devices to captivate the minds of young people and old people, too. It opens their minds to demon powers, and I'm very much against it. We've had girls come from homes where not only has astrology been used and looked into, but also other forms of the occult, such as black magic, were practiced."
                    Amy, San Martin, California.

"You cannot find out what is going to happen to you by going to any fortune teller or by reading your horoscope or by having someone read your stars or your palm or whatever, because that is not from God. If I don't know it's from Him, then it must be from Satan."   *Nancy, Reedley, California, Agape House.*

"It's like reincarnation; it makes you feel like you've got something, something to hold on to, but what do you have after you've got it? It doesn't make you grow as a personality. It stops you and it traps you into having to read it everyday. It really is garbage."

Anonymous.

Do you believe astrology works?

"I guess you could go goofing around or something just for kicks, you know. Like if it says you're going to find a nickel today, I'd believe it and start looking around for nickels, but I'm not really serious about it."   *Richard, Turlock, California, Rapping Post.*

"I just read my Bible."

Ronald, San Francisco, California.

"I know a guy that was an astrology master before he met Jesus. He could predict things by the stars. He said that astrology is valid. That by studying the stars and by understanding the stars, you could be convicted and completely convinced of the existence of Jesus Christ and the whole story of salvation—of us being sinners, and of our need to find God. But astrology has been perverted."   *Anonymous.*

"Astrology is good if it's not abused. They used astrology to find out where Christ was. They used astrology a lot of times in the Bible. It is a science but when you start worshipping a science, above God, it is wrong." *Maoch, Hayward, California, Children of God.*

"I believe that there might be some truth to it. As far as turning to it as a God as some people do, and living by it daily, I think that this is wrong."

Mildred, Los Angeles, California.

"Sure it works. That's how Satan gets his followers."

Cyd, San Francisco, California.

"I don't believe in astrology. I think the study of stars has led to idol worship."   *Chuck, Mississippi.*

"No, I don't believe in astrology. I think it's a very heavy deception that a lot of people have gotten into. We don't live under the signs of the stars—we live under the grace of God."
Kyle, Berkeley, California, Resurrection City.

"No. Astrology sure doesn't tell my future, or I don't guide my life by astrology. Only the Lord can do that. The book of Isaiah talks about astrology and it's just an abomination in the Lord's sight."
Troy, Atwater, California.

"No, I don't believe in it because God tells us what we have to be like in the Bible, and prophecy tells us what's going to happen."
Mark, Redwood City, California.

Chapter 10

IS THIS REALLY THE END?

"Christ Is Coming Soon" was the label that was stamped on furniture, blackboards, telephone poles, and even bathroom stalls in Berkeley in 1970.

That same slogan adorns this chapter.

What do you think about prophecy?

"As far as prophecy goes . . . let's take Jeane Dixon, for example. Now she correctly predicted the assassination of President Kennedy. Now, if that was from God, you'd think that that sort of information could have made some sort of difference as far as President Kennedy's death was concerned. What happened?— President Kennedy died anyway. He got assassinated. And, Jeane Dixon got another brownie point or whatever, and a few more thousand books that she was able to sell. Now, any sort of information that you get from God is always profitable. You'll always receive the end result of the information that you've been given."

Steve, Alameda, California, The Way.

"There are two kinds of prophecy as far as I know. I could be wrong. One kind is Bible prophecy about things to come in the future, and the other kind is the interpretation of tongues which is prophecy also in the present tense."

Nick, Turlock, California, Leader of His House.

"Prophecy is valid. It's a New Testament function in the Body of Christ. It comes forth in meetings that I've been to."

C. G., Mill Valley, California, Ivy House.

"About 4 years ago this one lady that I had seen for a couple of times said to my family, 'In the next few months and maybe a year, your family is to be a bridge of love to form many bridges of love.' From there my mother shared it with my brothers and sisters and since then we have found an unusual bond of love from that prophecy and we know that, that love comes from God."

Rock, Richmond, California, Christian House.

"I had a little talk with the Lord. The Lord said who I was gonna marry. I had a prophecy about six months ago, she didn't know I even liked her. I didn't think it was real. I tried to get away from her, and God kept bringing us closer and closer, and we'll be married a couple of months from now."

Steve, Turlock, California, The Christian House.

"Dreams, I'm not sure, but prophecies, yes. There was one in San Bruno at a revival and the man didn't know me and he said, 'Sister, I saw you in a bison dancing with a tambourine, do you play the tambourine?' He said the Lord said that your ministry is going to be a ministry of joy and that when people see your joy that you show forth, they will come to know Jesus." *Shelley, San Mateo, California.*

"I believe in prophecy, but I do think you have to watch it, because the Lord said that there would be false prophets arising, and it also says in the Bible to test the spirits and to see if it is of God. And so I think that you have to really make sure that it is of God, and if it is of God, then I believe it."

Shauna, San Jose, California, Agape House.

"I've heard some prophecies and I believe they're from the Lord. Of course, obviously not all prophecies are from the Lord—for instance, Jeane Dixon. Our spirits will testify and our knowledge of the Lord; if we know the Lord we'll be able to tell if these prophecies are from Him. . . . Before I was born again, being a Christian was just kind of an outward Christian being a trip. The Devil came to me and told me some really heavy stuff. The Lord didn't really let me get deceived even though I was not really calling the Lord. Now that I have become a Christian, the Lord has really told me some stuff and it has come true."

Steve, Mountain View, California.

"The Bible says, despise not prophecy, but urge it. All things are good unto God. Prophecy says that it can also be judged: you can tell whether the prophecy is from God or from man. The human heart can make up their own prophecy, but when true prophecy comes from God, it's always fulfilled; it always comes true."

Daniel, Campbell, California, Maranatha House.

"I think that if it's coming from the Spirit it's valid; if it's coming from the flesh, it's an abomination to the Christian community. I've been in meetings where I've seen both happen, and if it's coming from God, it rings true with your spirit, but that coming from the flesh is an abomination."

Kyle, Berkeley, California, Resurrection City.

Do you think Jesus is coming again soon?

"Very shortly. I think we are in the last days."

Kyle, Berkeley, California, Resurrection City.

"Jesus said that no man knows the hour or day; maybe you could know the month or the year, or something. Jesus said to look at the signs of the time. I

124

personally feel that the world really can't last too much longer. There's too much conflict and strife, and it's too easy to blow up the world. He said there'd be earthquakes and famines, and all kinds of things in the last days, that are happening right now. It's foolish to set any kind of date, but I'm looking for His return anytime."   *C. G., Mill Valley, California, Ivy House.*

"God gave us a few prophecies, and He named a few things that would happen prior to His coming back; and a lot of things are taking place right now that He prophesied: such as all the wars and strife everywhere. There's no place that's without it now. The main thing is when the Gospel will be preached through all the world, as He said, every part of the world will hear it, and that's going to be coming soon."

    Ben, Vallejo, California, New Disciples of Jesus.

"Well, Matthew says, no man will know the day or the hour, but we're not going to be ignorant of the signs of His coming, and I think it's pretty apparent that He's coming soon, but—who knows?"

    Troy, Atwater, California.

"I think Jesus will return probably in about 10 or 20 years—I mean I don't know, man. It's too much for me."   *Tim, Menlo Park, California.*

"Very soon, probably, I see the year 1971 just about right."   *Neil, Detroit, Michigan.*

"Within thirty years."
    Ken, Spokane, Washington, Maranatha House.

"Yes, it's real, it's where it's at today. I think there's nothing standing in the way of the Second Coming of Christ; because, like I said before, the prophecies are being fulfilled: like wars, floods, earthquakes. I know that we've always been able to say that there are these things, but there has been such an increase in these things. Yeah, He's coming soon."

Eugene, New York, New York.

"Personally, I think Christ will return to the earth within 15-20 years, depending on what happens."

Daniel, San Jose, California, Maranatha House.

"I feel He'll be here within 2 to 20 years. He could come tomorrow but it might be 20 years."

Gary, San Francisco, California.

"I believe Christ will return in this generation."

Dennis, Whittier, California, Christian House.

"Oh, just my own personal opinion: I would say within the next 15 or 20 years."

Bill, San Pablo, California.

"My personal opinion is that it will be within the next 40 years. Other people think it will be a lot sooner; some say, 'No, it will be longer.' "

Teresa, San Mateo, The Way Inn.

"When He gets good and ready."

Danny, Redwood City, California, House of Manna.

Do you think there will be a judgment day?

"The judgment day is the last day of the universe when everybody goes up and down."

Byron, Miami, Florida.

"I guess judgment is the day in which all mankind will be judged for their ways, whether they be evil or good." *John, Whittier, California, Agape Force.*

"The day of judgment is when the world is going to be judged for its sins—the White Throne Judgment. There are two judgments: the children of God are going to be judged, too, but not for their sins; and they will not stand in front of the White Throne Judgment—they will stand in front of the judgment of Christ to be judged according to their deeds, what they have done with their life; their idleness or whatever. But as far as the Judgment Day, that is when the world will be judged for their transgressions." *Nick, Turlock, California, Leader of His House.*

"The day of judgment is when the whole world has ended; and there'll be sorta like two judgment things: one for the Christians and one for the non-Christians. And the Christian will be naturally judged. They'll be rewarded on how they've done God's will and stuff. But the non-Christian will be judged and they will be condemned." *Alicia.*

"The judgment is when the great white throne and all the people that didn't know the Lord will be judged. The Christians that were taken up with Him on the day He comes before that—the Rapture—will be judged for their deeds, and they will be excluded, I believe, from the great white throne judgment."
George, Jacksonville, Illinois, Leader of His House.

"Actually, there's two judgments. There's one that the non-Christians will be judged and then there's the judgment seat of Christ that all the Christians will be judged for what they've done with their knowledge of Christ." *Sandra, Sunnyvale, California.*

"The day of judgment is happening right now the Lord is slowly closing the gates here and the numbers are being decided and those who get their names in the book of life are going to do it and those who don't are not going to do it and it's going to work down to the day of judgment. I believe it's going to come out and I believe that 60 or 65 percent are going to make it and 30 or 35 are not going to make it. This is a revelation that comes to me from the Lord. Every knee shall bow to the name of Jesus Christ."

Neil, San Francisco, California, Still Water Store.

Do you believe in Hell?

"Every single person will be judged on the day of judgment; the Bible says so. Every mouth shall confess that Jesus is Lord. Every person will be judged. If you come up before the judgment seat and you haven't got the blood of Jesus Christ cleansing you from your sins, then there's only one other place you can go, Hell."

Daniel, San Jose, California, Maranatha House.

"The day of judgment is when Jesus will come back and all the people whose names are in the Lamb's Book of Life will be in Heaven, and the other people will be taken down to Hell. I think that the Christians won't be judged and only the non-Christians."

Kristal, Turlock, California.

"The day of judgment is when everyone will come forth in front of God, and all of his works, be they good or bad, will be judged; and if his name isn't found in the Book of Life, the Bible is specific that he will be cast into Hell." *Anonymous.*